Vegan Pasta

Text and photographs by Clémence Catz

GRUB STREET | LONDON

Published in 2022 by
Grub Street
4 Rainham Close
London
SW11 6SS

Email: food@grubstreet.co.uk
Web: www.grubstreet.co.uk
Twitter: @grub_street
Facebook: Grub Street Publishing

Copyright this English language edition © Grub Street 2022

Copyright © 2020 Éditions Solar, un département d'Edi8, Paris
Published originally in French as *Pasta Vegan*
Photography Clémence Catz
Page design by Myriam Bell Design, UK

A CIP catalogue record for this book is available from the British Library.

ISBN 978-1-911667-24-7

All rights reserved. Without limiting the rights under copyright reserved above, no part of this publication may be reproduced, stored in or introduced into a retrieval system, or transmitted, in any form or by any means (electronic, mechanical, photocopying, recording or otherwise) without the prior written permission of both the copyright owner and the above publisher of this book.

Printed and bound by Finidr in the Czech Republic

Contents

Healthy veggie pasta	4
The 7 commandments for successful fresh (and vegetable) pasta	7
Fresh pasta recipes	10
Vegetable noodles: how to make them	20
10 gourmet sauce toppings	24
Classics reinvented	34
Healthy pasta packed with vitamins	60
Inspirations from around the world	88
Chic creative recipes	114
Index of recipes	143
Index of ingredients	144

Healthy Veggie Pasta

Nutritious, comforting and inexpensive, pasta is popular with young and old alike all over the world – or almost all over. From China to Italy, from the United States (with its famous mac and cheese) to delicious Japanese soba, there are hundreds of traditional recipes. It's believed that its origins go back to the dawn of time – or more precisely to the beginning of the Neolithic period, with the first lasagne made by alternating layers of meat and pasta cut into pieces. Pasta is often a simple square meal based on meat and/or cheese.

But did you know that pasta can also be healthy and 100% plant-based, made with ingredients that are colourful and with interesting textures such as cashew nut butter to kale pesto, asparagus tempura or miso mayonnaise? That meat can be replaced by flavoursome ingredients such as soya, pulses, seitan or grains that are high in complete proteins? And fish can be swapped for surprising ingredients such as fresh or flaked seaweed?

That seasonal vegetables deliciously enhance a beautiful pasta dish, whether added raw, chopped up, mixed in, roasted or creamed? That it's incredibly easy to make a plant-based ricotta or Parmesan using almonds with results that are full of flavour and nutrients? That you can make your own fresh pasta with wholemeal or gluten-free flours and colour it naturally with ingredients you have at home – from spinach to beetroot to fruit juice and ground superfoods? That it's even possible to make pasta without dough by using vegetables and just a potato peeler? And, above all, what's more delicious, creative and restorative than a wonderful vegetable pasta dish?

This book shows you how to prepare fifty truly different recipes, which you can make all year round with the wonderful seasonal produce that nature offers us. I've also included some recipes for fresh pasta, base recipes and gourmet toppings to add even more satisfaction. Throughout these pages, you'll discover great Italian classics revisited from a plant-based perspective, super healthy dishes full of colour and vitamins, inspirations from other places (from Asian noodles to crozets de Savoie and a wonderful revisited moussaka) not to mention creative and refined recipes for adventurous cooks who want to impress their guests.

Which pasta for which uses?

There are so many varieties of pasta and noodles that it's sometimes hard to know which to choose for which recipe – or how to make trofiette al ragù… without trofiette. Here's a little general guide arranged by pasta family so that you can make all the recipes in this book with what your favourite shop sells – as well as how to use the accessories that come with your pasta machine. In any case, feel free to adapt the recipes as you wish: if you feel like preparing the carbonara without spaghetti but with penne, the result will be just as good. Here's a useful tip: Asian noodles are sometimes specifically intended for particular dishes. When this is the case I suggest alternatives in the introduction or in the sidebar for the relevant recipes. Personally, I always have a variety of each kind in my pantry, as well as a few packets of udon or soba noodles – that way I can satisfy any craving. You can, of course, also use gluten-free or flavoured pasta.

- Fresh pasta (tagliatelle or linguine in particular) is ideal with light sauces.
- Medium-sized pasta (penne, fusilli, farfalle) goes well with thick sauces as well as those with chunks of vegetables – you can get both in the same mouthful.
- Long, wide pappardelle-type pasta goes best with creamy sauces.
- Small pasta with fun shapes and colours (orecchiette, conchigliette, trofiette) are perfect in salads as long as they're easy to eat with a fork: the smaller the vegetables, the smaller the size the pasta should be.
- When making stuffed pasta, think of cannelloni or large conchiglioni – just remember to choose the right type of stuffing as this kind of pasta breaks easily.
- For gratins, the macaroni used for America's famous mac and cheese can be substituted with conchigliette or other small pasta that evokes childhood memories.
- In soups, very small pasta (angel hair, vermicelli, alphabet pasta, orzo) is an easy and traditional option, but you can, of course, also dip into Asia's pantry and use udon, ramen or rice noodles.
- The latter are also delicious sautéed in a wok with vegetables and tofu and/or a light tamari-based sauce, or cold in a salad after quickly running the cooked noodles under a little cold water.
- We mustn't forget lasagne, a unique kind of pasta, which can be replaced by very thinly sliced or slightly pre-cooked strips of vegetables (cucumber, courgette, squash).
- Last but not least is a separate category: plant-based noodles, such as ones made with seaweed (konjac, kelp, sea spaghetti), which are more delicate and are served simply with a light sauce and with finely chopped herbs.

As deciding on the quantity of pasta per serving is quite a personal matter, I arbitrarily chose quantities I believe are consistent with usual consumption. Feel free to adapt the recipes to your tastes.

Buon appetito!

The 7 Commandments for Successful Fresh (and Vegetable) Pasta

> *Making fresh pasta isn't complicated, especially when you have the right ingredients and a few good tips. The result is incomparable and you can personalise your pasta by giving it the shape, colour and flavour you want: a pinch of saffron for a beautiful golden hue, lemon zest or a spoonful of dried tarragon for inimitable flavours… or lasagne just the right size to fit your dish. Here are some basic rules to remember:*

1. How to choose your flour

Artisanal pasta is usually made with durum wheat semolina, which is very popular in Italy as it is firmer and allows for that little al dente touch that we love. You can, of course, swap it for white flour or a half/half mix, but as I'm a great fan of old-fashioned, unprocessed wholemeal flour, I'd rather sacrifice a little sensory pleasure for the sake of ethics and nutrition – and besides, the flavour is so much better! So, I often choose wonderful spelt flour for my traditional recipes and I pick from the wide range of gluten-free grains available for the others. It's then important to enrich the pasta with natural texturing agents (flax or chia seeds, starch, psyllium), which make the resulting taste absolutely worth it.

If you prefer to stick to wheat flour (if only to start with), I recommend using Type 80 wheat flour, which will allow you to make wonderful semi-wholegrain pasta. It's best to choose flours milled by a miller, if possible one who's local and who uses quality grains – that way you'll enjoy fresh flour that's nutritious and tastes great. If this isn't an option, buy it from a shop that sells organic produce and in bulk to ensure that it hasn't been sitting on the shelves for months: and precisely because of this, avoid buying flour from supermarkets.

2. Make lovely egg-free pasta

To make 'traditional' fresh pasta, one egg is generally needed for every 100 g of wheat flour. For a 100% plant-based version, simply swap the egg for its weight in water, i.e. about 50 g. Preferably use lukewarm or water at room temperature, adding it little by little while mixing: when the dough comes together, add the olive oil and knead for 5 to 10 minutes by hand or in a food processor. The final result should be a soft but relatively firm dough that is not sticky, rather like Play-Doh. Don't worry if you need to add a little more water or flour during the kneading process: the humidity of the dough varies depending on the flour used, the temperature of the room and the method of kneading (by hand or in a food processor). Remember that quantities can be quite different when using gluten-free flours.

Never add salt to the dough, as small white spots will appear under the surface. You should only add salt to water used for cooking!

3. Don't skip the resting phase

This is an essential step for making successful fresh pasta and ensuring it will have a smooth texture when cooked. To stop your dough from drying out, wrap it in cling film and leave it on a worktop for 20 to 30 minutes. As it doesn't contain eggs, you don't need to leave it in the fridge, which would make it too hard to work with. Important: when you divide your dough to work it, leave the other pieces wrapped in cling film – or in a freezer bag – so that they don't dry out.

4. How to use a pasta machine

If you want to make tagliatelle or spaghetti, you'll find it hard to do without a dough sheeter or pasta machine; this simple, inexpensive device not only flattens the dough very finely, but also cuts it into strands or ribbons, or even into ravioli and pappardelle if you have the right accessories. If you prefer to work it by hand, you'll need a good rolling pin (although you'll find it hard to get the pasta as thin as with a pasta machine), a knife and lots of patience when it comes to cutting it. To use a pasta machine, first divide the dough into portions and flatten them slightly before feeding them

four or five times between the rollers of the machine that should be set to the widest setting. Fold the resulting sheets over themselves each time they are rolled as this helps the gluten to form and makes them more flexible and less fragile. Feed them through the pasta machine several times, increasing one notch at a time, until the desired thickness is reached (medium for tagliatelle, as thin as possible for ravioli and a little thinner for lasagne). Divide them in half lengthways before feeding them through with the specific accessory (tagliatelle, spaghetti, etc.). Don't worry if you have to lightly flour the dough before feeding it through the rollers of the pasta machine – and often before cutting it so that the pasta you're making separates well and doesn't stick together later. Good to know: a pasta machine can be used to roll out all types of dough – if you love Asian cuisine or oriental pastries you'll find that it pays for itself very quickly.

5. Drying fresh pasta

This is an important but not essential step, which allows the fresh pasta to not stick together and to have a good texture when cooked. Thirty minutes is usually enough: any longer and the pasta becomes brittle. However, if you wish to keep the pasta for a few days, you'll need to allow 24 hours for it to dry, and then handle it with care.

You don't need to invest in a pasta dryer, unless you're going to make pasta every day: just lay clean tea towels on a worktop or over the back of a chair. You can also place a floured (clean) broom handle between two tables. There are loads of tips!

6. How to keep pasta fresh (before cooking)

If you want to make dried pasta, you'll need to air dry it for 24 hours (see the previous point), then carefully store it in an airtight container on dry kitchen paper, making sure it's not at all damp. It can be kept for a few weeks. Another option – and simpler in my opinion – is to freeze it shaped, for example, into nests: you can then put them straight into boiling water, cooking for an additional 1 or 2 minutes.

7. Successful cooking

A few basic tips: make sure you use plenty of water and don't forget the salt – calculate 10 grams of salt per 100 grams of pasta in 1 litre of water. Stir once or twice gently with a fork to prevent the pasta from sticking together (don't bother adding oil to the water, it does absolutely nothing). Fresh pasta cooks very quickly, usually in around 3 minutes.

Fresh Pasta Recipes

Spelt tagliatelle

> This is a simple but delicious recipe that will give you all the benefits of spelt's many properties; it's low in gluten and easy to digest, and it's high in complete proteins, phosphorus, magnesium and vitamin B. In addition, as it's also made with durum wheat flour, when it's cooked it stays al dente. Cook the tagliatelle at the last minute and serve them at once with walnut pesto (see recipe, p. 31) or with a drizzle of hazelnut oil and plant-based Parmesan (see recipe, p. 24).

Serves 3 to 4
Prep time: 25 minutes
Resting time: 30 minutes
Cooking time: 4 minutes

200 g spelt flour, plus extra for the rolling process
100 g fine durum wheat flour
2 tbsp olive oil

Mix the spelt and durum wheat flours together in a mixing bowl. Add 150 ml of warm water and mix with a spatula until the mixture comes together. Then add the olive oil and knead for 5 to 10 minutes by hand or in a food processor. Leave to stand, wrapped in cling film, for about 30 minutes. Then divide the dough into 6 pieces, flatten the first one slightly and feed it through the pasta machine several times set to the widest setting (see the 7 commandments for successful fresh pasta, p. 8).

Now, before feeding the dough through each time, turn the dial to the next narrowest setting until you reach the setting for tagliatelle (usually 5 or 6, but check the instructions of your machine).

Dust the resulting sheet well with flour and feed it gently through the machine using the tagliatelle attachment. Dry the tagliatelle without overlapping them for about 30 minutes before cooking for 2 to 3 minutes in a large saucepan of boiling water.

Real gnocchi di patate

This is the real recipe for gnocchi, which is made just with potatoes and flour. The three rules to follow are: choose floury potatoes (they're less watery); drain them for a long time to dry them well; use as little flour as necessary – it'll be a bit harder to work the dough but the gnocchi will be so much better.

Serves 4
Prep time: 30 minutes
Resting time: 30 minutes
Cooking time: 30 minutes

1 kg floury potatoes (Bintje, Marabel, Caesar, Russet, etc.)
250 to 300 g T65 flour, plus extra for dusting the worktop
½ tsp fine salt
Vegetable oil

Bring a large saucepan of water to a boil. Brush the skin of the potatoes and cook until tender, 15 to 20 minutes. Pour off the water and leave them in a colander to dry for 30 minutes before peeling them. Crush them in a bowl or straight on a floured worktop with a fork or potato ricer, then add the flour and salt. Mix together by hand and knead, adding more flour until you have a nice smooth, non-sticky ball. Stop kneading as soon as it's smooth as this will avoid it becoming sticky.

Roll the dough into ropes about 1.5 cm in diameter on a well-floured worktop. Cut into 2-cm wide pieces and lightly press each one on the tines of a fork to curl them. Don't worry if you have to add a little more flour while you make the gnocchi as this stops them sticking to the worktop. Set them aside on a lightly floured tray or large plate without overlapping them.

When all the gnocchi are ready, bring a large saucepan of salted water to a boil, add the gnocchi and cook for 3 to 4 minutes, or until they rise to the surface. Use a skimmer to take them out and put them in a dish. Drizzle with a little vegetable oil. You can cook them in various batches to avoid the gnocchi sticking together in the saucepan. This can happen if you cook too many at a time. Serve immediately.

Tip

The Italian technique for cleaning your hands after kneading the gnocchi? Rub them together with a little more flour, and that's it!

Chickpea flour trofie

Trofie is a typical pasta from the region of Liguria. They have an irregular twisty shape, making sauces cling to them particularly well – and are often served with pesto. They're usually made by hand, without a pasta machine. This is my gluten-free version made with chickpea flour. It's delicious with fresh tomato sauce, aubergine caviar or with diced and roasted pumpkin.

Serves 4
Prep time: 1 hour
Cooking time: 8 minutes
Resting time: 30 minutes

30 g flax seeds
300 g chickpea flour
60 g arrowroot powder
20 ml olive oil
Salt

Process the flax seeds and mix with 180 ml of hot water. Leave to stand for 10 minutes.

Mix the chickpea flour with the arrowroot in a large bowl. Make a well in the centre, pour in the flax and water mixture. Mix with a spatula until the texture is sandy, then add the olive oil and knead for 5 minutes by hand until you have a nice ball of dough that is soft but firm. Leave to rest for 20 minutes wrapped in cling film or in a freezer bag.

Pick off small balls of dough about 1 cm in diameter (keep the rest wrapped in cling film to stop it drying out). Warm them between the palms of your hands and roll them forwards on the worktop then backwards diagonally to form an irregular twist with pointed ends. Set aside on a clean tea towel. When all the trofie are ready, bring a generous amount of salted water to a boil. Put in the fresh pasta and stir gently with a fork so that it doesn't stick together. Cook for about 8 minutes then drain, mix with the sauce and serve.

Tip

There are lots of tutorials on the Internet for learning how to roll trofie correctly. You just have to get the hang of it.

Quinoa and lemon lasagne

There's not much work involved in making fresh lasagne as you just make the 'sheets' without having to cut them afterwards and, in addition, they're much more melt-in-the-mouth than shop-bought ones. Cut them to fit the shape of your dish, and flavour them as you wish: this pretty golden lasagne made with quinoa flour and lemon zest is extraordinary with courgettes and a béchamel sauce perfumed with a little basil pesto.

Serves 4 to 6
Prep time: 30 minutes
Resting time: 30 minutes

120 g T80 wheat flour, plus a little extra for dusting
80 g quinoa
Zest of 1 organic lemon
2 tbsp olive oil
1 pinch of turmeric (optional for colour)

Mix the wheat and quinoa flours in a bowl with the finely chopped lemon zest and turmeric if using. Add 100 ml of warm water and stir until the mixture comes together. Add the olive oil and knead for 10 minutes by hand or for 5 minutes in a food processor. Set aside for 30 minutes wrapped in cling film.

Cut the dough into four pieces. Leave three wrapped in cling film (or in a freezer bag) and flatten the first one slightly between your palms. Set your pasta machine to the widest setting and feed the dough through it three or four times, folding the dough in between each time you feed it through (you can also fold it in thirds, like a wallet, which will give you nice rectangular sheets of lasagne). Lightly flour the dough on both sides and turn the dial to the next setting each time you feed it through (at this stage, there's no need to fold the dough over on itself) until you reach setting 6. When the sheet gets too long or becomes too fragile, cut it in half or to fit your dish. Set the finished sheets aside on a clean tea towel, without overlapping them. You can use them as soon as they're ready. There's no need to precook anything, just assemble the lasagne and cook for 30 minutes in a hot oven.

Variations

Flavour the fresh dough with:
- 2 teaspoons of dried herbs
- (tarragon, chives, herbes de Provence or oregano)
- 1 heaped teaspoon of spices (cumin, curry, turmeric, cardamom)
- 1 pinch of Espelette or Cayenne pepper
- Zest of 1 orange (delicious with pumpkin)
- Try making your pasta colourful too! (see recipe p. 18)

Colourful pasta

> *It's easy to customise your pasta with natural colouring, and it's a delicious way to enhance it with nutrients from vegetables and superfoods. Don't worry if you need to adjust the proportions of water and flour according to the consistency obtained.*

For pink pasta (per person)

Mix 100 grams of flour with 50 ml of beetroot juice (or a piece of beetroot blended with water) in a bowl. When the mixture starts to come together, add 1 tablespoon of olive oil and form a ball of soft dough, knead for 5 to 10 minutes.

For yellow pasta (per person)

Mix 100 grams of flour with 50 ml of warm water and 1 heaped teaspoon of turmeric in a bowl. When the mixture starts to come together, add 1 tablespoon of olive oil and form a ball of soft dough, knead for 5 to 10 minutes.

For green pasta (per person)

Put 1 handful of spinach (stems removed) in a saucepan. Cover and wilt it with 1 or 2 tablespoons of water. Drain for a long time to dry out the spinach, then blend 30 grams of it with 40 ml of water. Mix the purée obtained with 100 grams of flour in a bowl. When the mixture starts to come together, add 1 tablespoon of olive oil and form a ball of soft dough, knead for 5 to 10 minutes.

For black pasta (per person)

Mix 100 grams of flour with 50 ml of warm water and 1 teaspoon of activated charcoal (available in the health section of organic food shops or at the chemist) in a bowl. When the mixture starts to come together, add 1 tablespoon of olive oil and form a ball of soft dough, knead for 5 to 10 minutes.

For purple pasta (per person)

Mix 100 grams of flour with 50 ml of blueberry juice. When the mixture starts to come together, add 1 tablespoon of olive oil and form a ball of soft dough, knead for 5 to 10 minutes.

Other variations you can try…

- ▶ Yellow pasta: butternut squash, chickpea flour, saffron
- ▶ Orange pasta: carrot juice, tomato paste, pumpkin, red lentils, achiote infusion
- ▶ Red pasta: cherry or cranberry juice, red beans
- ▶ Pink and purple pasta: nerone or black rice, blackcurrant juice plus 1 teaspoon lemon juice, rhubarb (cooked unpeeled), hibiscus infusion
- ▶ Blue pasta: cultivated blueberries, spirulina, red cabbage decoction
- ▶ Green pasta: cooked and blended broccoli, arugula, pistachio butter, matcha tea

Vegetable Noodles, How to Make Them

Veggie noodles are a great way to eat more plant-based food while lowering your carb intake and enhancing your dishes – in a gluten-free way, of course. Very easy to make, no equipment is required and they can be prepared in the blink of an eye. They only take a few minutes to cook (very useful when it comes to vegetables such as squash or sweet potatoes) and can be prepared in a thousand and one ways. It's a great idea for children too, as they'll suddenly find vegetables much more appealing.

How to make veggie noodles

The most classic and easily adaptable kinds are tagliatelle and spaghetti. Make them in several ways:

- ▶ Use a mandoline: Most mandolines have special julienne blades that let you make perfectly even slices. By running the chosen vegetable lengthwise over it, you'll have beautiful spaghetti in no time. They'll be a bit stiff at this stage but will soften when cooked. Even without the perfect blade, you can still set your mandoline to a fairly thin thickness; slice the vegetable into strips (watch your fingers!), then cut tagliatelle to the desired width or, if you've got the time and the energy, into spaghetti.
- ▶ Use a vegetable peeler: Instead of just peeling your vegetables, keep cutting the flesh into strips – this will make 'pappardelle', which you can then cut into thinner strips with a knife to make tagliatelle. You can also use a vegetable peeler with a serrated blade, designed

for julienning vegetables, but that works perfectly well to make vegetable noodles: in my opinion, this is one of the most efficient and least cumbersome methods to make beautiful spaghetti at a very low cost, but it does require a little more time than using a mandoline or a Spiralizer®, as you have to turn the vegetables regularly on all sides to obtain uniform noodles.

▶ Use a Spiralizer®: This is the 'luxury' option, yet it's inexpensive and will pay for itself very quickly – especially if you're like me and you eat veggie noodles several times a week. There are all kinds available: small and manual, electric or professional (some major brands of multifunction food processors come with a Spiralizer® accessory). Depending on the appliance you have, you can choose from various types of cuts (fettuccine, spaghetti, angel hair, ribbons, etc.) and use a wide variety of vegetables, from the most tender to very hard ones. A Spiralizer® makes beautiful, soft, wavy noodles with a turn of a crank and is the perfect gadget if you don't have much room on your worktop. Remember, it generally needs vegetables to have a certain diameter to get caught by the blades, and some gadgets have a bit of trouble with the hardest vegetables. Check this before you buy!

▶ Use a pencil-sharpener type of Spiralizer®: This little gadget, which takes up little more space than a peeler, works just like a peeler and effortlessly makes pretty good wavy spaghetti, although they can be slightly less aesthetic than those made with a classic Spiralizer®. It's okay for using occasionally, but it's not what I'd recommend for regular use as it's a bit tedious to handle – a vegetable peeler that juliennes is a better option, and your wrists won't get so tired.

Which vegetables are best?

Most firm vegetables (and fruits) can be made into spaghetti. Here are some ideas: squash and pumpkin, beetroot, carrots, cucumbers, apples, sweet potatoes, large radishes, cabbage, turnips, peppers…and the most famous: courgetti (the nickname for courgette spaghetti), which, thanks to being firm but not too soft, also make pretty tagliatelle – and even very versatile sheets of lasagne.

How do you cook veggie noodles?

Many vegetables can be eaten raw, in salads, with a vinaigrette and gourmet toppings, but my favourite way to prepare them is to cook them al dente in a frying pan or wok – perfect for vegetables that only need a quick cooking time (courgettes, cabbage, radishes, etc.). For others, start by cooking them in the same way, then add 2 to 3 tablespoons of water before covering and leaving them to cook for a few more minutes over a low heat. Or you can steam vegetables, which allows them to retain their vitamins and keeps them crunchy. Remember, no matter which method you choose, take them off the heat when the vegetables are still a little firm as they continue to cook for a few minutes. I usually calculate a minimum cooking time, then leave off the heat for 3 to 5 minutes (uncovered) before finishing and serving.

Some ideas

Prepare your veggie noodles like real pasta, adding oil and herbs, sauces you like, small crunchy seeds or plant-based cheese, etc. and eat them quickly, before they get too soft.

Try courgetti with an uncooked tomato sauce (see recipe p. 68) or a cooked one, with plant-based Parmesan and toasted sunflower seeds; butternut spaghetti sautéed in coconut oil with 1 or 2 minced shallots, then cooked for 5 minutes, covered, over low heat with orange juice and served with citrus gremolata (see recipe p. 30); an apple and beetroot salad with walnut pesto (see recipe p. 31), courgette and pepper spaghetti with almond and basil pesto (see recipe p. 27), steamed carrots with roasted chickpeas (see recipe p. 29), etc. You'll have fun making sheets of lasagne with squash or courgettes, or vegetable patties with veggie spaghetti and a little added potato starch.

Tip

When you make veggie noodles with a Spiralizer®, vegetable peeler or mandoline there's usually a little waste as the ends of the vegetables used are left over as you've been holding them and they can't be sliced any more, or bits are left in the gadget. I store these small pieces in the freezer and make a good multi-vegetable soup when I've accumulated enough.

10 Gourmet Sauces Toppings

Plant-based Parmesan

This plant-based Parmesan made with oilseeds is not only delicious and easy to make, but also very high in selenium thanks to the Brazil nuts. My suggestion: try several brands of malted yeast and find your favourite as they all have different flavours.

Makes 1 small bowl
Prep time: 5 minutes

60 g cashew nuts
30 g Brazil nuts
3 tbsp malted yeast
1 scant tsp sea salt
½ level tsp garlic powder

Process the cashew and Brazil nuts in batches to a coarse powder. Add the remaining ingredients and pulse for a moment. Store in an airtight container in the fridge and use within 2 weeks.

Variation

Use only cashew nuts, or a cashew-macadamia combination.

Roasted tomato sauce

Here's a delicious version of traditional passata, a tomato sauce that's essential for any good pasta dish. In this recipe, the tomatoes are roasted in the oven for a long time before being cooked in a saucepan with very few additional ingredients – this really brings out their flavour. Choose beautiful, ripe tomatoes: those at the end of the season are often the best.

Serves 4
Prep time: 12 minutes
Cooking time: 1 hour and 20 minutes

8 very ripe tomatoes
50 ml olive oil, plus 2 tbsp
2-3 garlic cloves, or as desired
2 shallots
1 large pinch of raw cane sugar
5 or 6 basil leaves
Salt, pepper

Wash the tomatoes, cut them in half and remove most of the seeds. Place them on a baking tray lined with greaseproof paper, skin-side down. Drizzle with 2 tablespoons of olive oil and roast for about 1 hour at 180°C (gas mark 4). When you take them out, drain the tomatoes in a colander (you can use the juice in a soup, stock or sauce base) and then peel. Heat the olive oil in a heavy-bottomed pan and add the peeled, sliced degermed garlic and the peeled sliced shallots. Cook and stir for 2 minutes, then add the tomatoes and sugar and cook for about 20 minutes over a low heat, stirring occasionally, or until the consistency of the sauce is to your taste – you can give it a quick whiz in a blender if you prefer a smooth sauce. Add the basil, salt and pepper.

Garlic croutons

> These small grilled croutons are flavoured with garlic, herbes de Provence and Espelette pepper. Super easy to prepare, they're a great way to recycle hard stale bread and are delicious on a pasta dish with a creamy sauce or passata, adding a lovely crunchy touch.

For 1 large bowl of croutons
Prep time: 10 minutes
Cooking time: 12 minutes

150 g stale bread
3 tbsp olive oil
2 cloves garlic
2 tsp herbes de Provence or oregano
½ tsp Espelette pepper
½ tsp sea salt

Preheat the oven to 200°C (gas mark 6).

Mix the olive oil with the peeled, degermed and crushed garlic, herbes de Provence, Espelette pepper and salt in a large bowl. Add the bread, cut into small 1.5-cm cubes. Use your hands to toss them until well coated all over.

Spread the croutons (without overlapping them) on a baking sheet lined with greaseproof paper and bake for about 12 minutes, or until crisp and golden. Use within 3 days.

Almond and basil pesto

Here's a 100% vegetable version of this classic Italian pasta dish: lots of basil, almonds and cashew nuts with their sweet flavour and slightly grainy texture, garlic of course, and a hint of malted yeast for a cheesy taste. Use it on all summer vegetable pasta dishes.

For 1 jam jar
Prep time: 10 minutes

- 3 large handfuls of basil leaves (1 good bunch, about 50 g)
- 40 g unpeeled almonds
- 40 g cashew nuts
- 2 cloves garlic
- ½ tsp salt
- 2 tbsp malted yeast
- 80 g olive oil

Wash the basil leaves, gently dry them and put in the jar of a blender with the almonds, cashew nuts, peeled and degermed garlic cloves and salt. Blend for about 10 seconds to obtain a mixture that's still a bit coarse in texture. Add the malted yeast, blend to incorporate, then drizzle in the olive oil while blending. Taste and adjust the seasoning if necessary, or add a little more olive oil (see note below). Store in an airtight jar in the fridge and use within 2 weeks.

Comment

This very nutty pesto is quite thick; you can add some extra olive oil to make it more fluid, or thin it with a little water to the desired consistency.

Cashew cream

What would vegetable pasta be without cashew cream? This simple, incredibly creamy dish that has a delicious cheese flavour, can be prepared in a blender and will enhance any pasta dish.

For 1 bowl (pasta for 4 people)
Soaking time: 3-4 hours
Prep time: 5 minutes

- 100 g cashew nuts, soaked in cold water for 3 to 4 hours
- 1 tbsp lemon juice
- 1 scant tsp onion granules
- ⅓ tsp garlic powder
- 2 tbsp malted yeast
- ½ tsp sea salt
- A few turns of the pepper mill

Rinse the cashew nuts. Place them in the jar of a blender with 125 ml of water and the other ingredients. Blend for a long time to a smooth and lump-free cream. Add a little water if you want a smoother texture. Taste and adjust the seasoning if necessary by adding a little salt and pepper or a pinch of yeast for a more cheesy flavour.

Tip

If you forget to soak the cashew nuts, here's what to do: bring a small saucepan of water to the boil, remove from the heat and soak the cashew nuts for 15 to 20 minutes. All you have to do now is rinse and blend.

Variation

Feel free to personalise the recipe according to the ingredients it's accompanying: 1 teaspoon of smoked paprika, chopped chives, lemon zest or a little miso or tamari…

Roasted chickpeas

Super easy to prepare, these oven-roasted chickpeas make a delicious crunchy topping for most pasta dishes, or even as they are as nibbles. This is my favourite variation, made with thyme and cumin.

For 1 bowl
Prep time: 5 minutes
Cooking time: 25 minutes

200 g cooked chickpeas (rinsed and drained if from a jar)
1 tbsp olive oil
1 heaped tsp dried thyme
1 scant tsp ground cumin
1 generous pinch of Espelette pepper
Salt, pepper

Preheat the oven to 200°C (gas mark 6). Put the chickpeas in a bowl, add the olive oil, thyme and spices, salt and pepper. Mix well. Spread them out loosely on a baking tray lined with greaseproof paper and roast for 20 to 25 minutes, or until the chickpeas are lightly browned. Allow to cool completely before eating (you can also eat them warm).

Variation

Sweet spices (turmeric, cinnamon, ginger, cardamom), orange or lemon zest, herbs of your choice (tarragon, herbes de Provence) or a dash of tamari.

Gremolata

Gremolata is a Milanese condiment made with parsley, garlic and lemon. Revitalising, bright and super-charged, it's also a great way to dress up a dish made with fresh pasta. Here's a version with oranges that's lovely in winter with squash and root vegetables – great in summer with courgettes, for example, and all you need to do is simply use lemon instead of the orange. Prepare gremolata in small quantities and eat it the same day. At a pinch you can eat it the next day, but the flavour fades quickly.

Serves 3 to 4
Prep time: 5 minutes

- ½ bunch parsley
- 1 or 2 cloves garlic (depending on their size and how garlicky you want it)
- Zest of 1 organic lemon
- Zest of ½ organic orange
- 2 tbsp olive oil
- 1 pinch of salt

Finely chop the parsley and the peeled and degermed garlic. Use a fine grater or Microplane® to zest the orange and/or lemon. Mix everything together in a small bowl, add salt and olive oil. Store in a jar in the fridge and use within 48 hours.

Variation

Create your own recipes based on combinations of herbs and citrus fruits: orange and coriander, basil and lemon, mint or lemon balm and lime… You can also swap the garlic for chopped shallot and/or enhance the mixture with crushed pink peppercorns.

Walnut pesto

This indulgent, full-bodied pesto is ideal with wholemeal pasta dishes made with spelt, buckwheat or quinoa, or with winter vegetables. Try replacing the parsley with other herbs (fresh coriander, chives, tarragon) and swap the brown miso for white miso, which is very light and silky.

For 1 bowl
Prep time: 10 minutes

60 g walnuts
1 clove garlic
1 heaped tbsp finely chopped parsley
50 g olive oil
2 tsp barley or brown rice

Chop the nuts more or less finely depending on the desired result. Finely crush the peeled and degermed garlic clove. Mix the walnuts with the garlic and chopped parsley, add the olive oil while mixing or blending. Finish with the miso, mix well and taste, add a little more parsley or miso if you wish. You can also slightly increase the amount of olive oil.

Tip

Prepare this pesto in small quantities as the nuts oxidise quickly once chopped and it'll only keep in the fridge for 2 to 3 days.

Tamari toasted seeds

> *This simple recipe is actually my favourite homemade appetiser, recycled here as a crunchy topping. Flavour the seeds with whatever takes your fancy and enjoy the topping over a dish of pasta with Alfredo sauce (see recipe p. 48) or an Asian noodle soup.*

Makes 1 small bowl
Prep time: 5 minutes

25 g almonds
40 g cashew nuts
30 g sunflower seeds
3 tbsp tamari
1 tsp cumin seeds
1 generous pinch of garlic powder
1 scant tsp onion granules
1 tsp dried thyme or herbes de Provence
½ tsp smoked paprika, etc.

Dry roast the seeds, almonds and cashew nuts in a small frying pan, heavy-bottomed if possible, for 3 to 4 minutes, stirring often, until they start to brown. Add the herbs or spices you've decided on. Sauté for another minute, then remove from heat and add the tamari. Mix briskly, tip onto a plate and leave to cool, then chop more or less finely depending on the desired result. Store in an airtight container at room temperature and use within 3 to 4 days.

White bean béchamel sauce

In this astonishing béchamel sauce, the butter, milk and flour called for in the traditional recipe are replaced by a simple, fragrant white bean cream, packed with beneficial proteins. Most importantly, it can be prepared in the blink of an eye, which isn't often the case with pulse-based recipes. Lovely in lasagne (see recipe p. 16) or cannelloni dishes, it also enhances vegetable pasta dishes.

For 1 small bowl (pasta for 4 people)
Prep time: 10 minutes

- 200 g cooked white beans (homemade or in a jar)
- 1 tbsp lemon juice
- 2 tsp malted yeast
- 1 pinch of garlic powder
- 1 pinch of nutmeg
- 1 tsp vegetable stock powder (or ½ cube, crumbled)
- Salt, pepper

Rinse and drain the white beans if they're from a jar. Put them in a blender with the lemon juice, yeast, garlic and nutmeg, and season with salt (lightly) and pepper. Prepare 90 ml of stock with the vegetable stock powder and pour over the above ingredients. Blend to obtain a smooth fluid cream, adding a little stock if you wish. Use at once.

Tip

It's best to eat it at once as it tends to dry out; if it does, add a little stock and give it another quick whiz.

Classics Reinvented

Spaghetti, seitan 'meatballs' and tomato sauce

A great classic of the Italian trattoria, spaghetti with meatballs is fortunately not off limits for vegans: this melt-in-the-mouth, very flavoursome and wonderfully comforting version, with seitan and red beans, is every bit as good as the original. Try replacing the red beans with chickpeas, and use homemade or shop-bought seitan, but keep in mind that each seitan has its own texture and the result will be a little different each time – add a little potato starch to the dough if it seems too wet, and a little tomato paste and tamari if it's too dry.

Serves 4
Prep time: 25 minutes
Cooking time: 20 minutes

For the 'meatballs':
280 g seitan
2 shallots
1 clove garlic
3 tbsp olive oil
1 tbsp tomato paste
1 tsp smoked paprika
2 tsp tamari
200 g cooked kidney beans
2 tbsp plant-based Parmesan
   (see recipe p. 24)
or 1 tbsp malted yeast plus
   1 tbsp ground almonds
2 tbsp finely chopped parsley
Salt, pepper

Tomato sauce for 4 people
   (see recipe p. 25)

400 g spaghetti

Prepare the 'meatballs': peel the shallots, peel and degerm the garlic. Chop them up, fry for 3 to 4 minutes in 1 tablespoon of olive oil, then add the tomato paste, paprika and tamari. Stir and take off the heat. Cut the seitan into pieces and put in a blender with the beans (rinsed and drained if canned or from a jar), the plant-based Parmesan and the fried shallots and garlic. Season with salt and pepper. Blend in short bursts to chop the mixture.

Add the parsley then blend again quickly so that everything comes together. Shape the meatballs with wet hands, then cook them for 6 to 7 minutes all over in a non-stick pan with the remaining olive oil. Add the tomato sauce and reheat it with the meatballs.

To cook the spaghetti, follow the instructions on the packet. Drain and serve with the meatballs in tomato sauce. Sprinkle with a little plant-based Parmesan if you wish.

Cannelloni, chard and soya curds

These cannelloni take a little time to prepare, but you'll learn how to make your own tofu with soya milk. Don't throw out the whey as it's full of protein and delicious in soups or stocks.

Serves 3 to 4
Prep time: 40 minutes
Cooking time: 30 minutes
Resting time: 25 minutes

1 litre soya milk
3 tbsp lemon juice
3 tbsp apple cider vinegar
2 tbsp olive oil
250 g chard leaves
2 shallots
1 clove garlic
8 to 10 cannelloni
40 g sunflower seeds
100 ml plant-based cream
1 tbsp breadcrumbs
Salt, pepper

Prepare the tofu: pour the milk into a large saucepan and bring to the boil. Add the lemon juice and vinegar, stir once or twice with a wooden spoon and leave for 15 minutes off the heat to curdle. Large lumps should have formed in the milk and have separated from the whey. If this hasn't happened, bring to the boil again and add 2 tablespoons of vinegar or lemon juice before curdling again. Pour the mixture into a fine sieve lined with cheesecloth and place over a bowl. Leave to drain for 10 to 15 minutes, pressing lightly with a wooden spoon if necessary: the whey will drain into the bowl and the tofu will stay in the sieve.

In the meantime, wash and chop the chard leaves and fry in olive oil for 10 minutes with the garlic and the peeled and chopped shallots. Season with salt and pepper. Bring a generous amount of water to a boil and cook the pasta following the instructions on the packet. Stir occasionally to stop it from sticking together.

Preheat the oven to 180°C (gas mark 4).

Dry roast the sunflower seeds for a few minutes in a frying pan, then roughly chop them. Mix the tofu with the chard and ¾ of the sunflower seeds. Use a small spoon or piping bag to stuff the cannelloni. Drizzle with cream and sprinkle with breadcrumbs and the remaining sunflower seeds. Bake for about 20 minutes, adding a little more cream during cooking if necessary. Serve hot.

Note

The curds in this recipe are similar to silken tofu. For firm tofu, just press on it harder and for longer; put a weight on a plate for example, or use a tofu press (you can find them online or in specialised shops). Store it in its whey and use it within 3 days.

Linguine alla puttanesca

Puttanesca is a traditional sauce made with anchovies, capers and olives. There are no anchovies in this recipe as I've used dulse instead; a beautiful red seaweed with a slightly briny and subtle hazelnut flavour, it's particularly high in protein, amino acids and trace elements. It's amazing and particularly spectacular paired with capers and olives, but you can, of course, use with any other seaweed of your choice instead – sea lettuce or sea spaghetti, for example. Dulse is commonly found in the fresh section of organic grocery shops. If yours doesn't have it, use dried seaweed that comes in a packet, which has to be rehydrated before you use it.

Serves 4
Prep time: 15 minutes
Cooking time: 10 minutes

60 g fresh dulse
400 g linguine
3 tbsp olive oil
2 cloves garlic
50 g capers (in salt or in brine)
100 g Kalamata olives (or other good black olives)

Put the dulse in a bowl and cover generously with cold water, stir with your fingertips and leave for 5 minutes. Drain the water and repeat the process, then rinse and drain. Set aside.

To cook the pasta, follow the instructions on the packet.

Meanwhile, rinse the capers if they're in salt and dry them quickly with kitchen paper or a clean tea towel. Peel, degerm and finely chop the garlic. Pit the olives and slice them.

Heat the oil in a frying pan and fry the garlic for 3 minutes. Add the capers and olives, cook and stir for another minute, then set aside.

Drain the pasta and mix it gently with the seaweed and olive mixture, serve immediately.

Skillet lasagne, roasted tomatoes and white bean béchamel

Never heard of 'skillet lasagne'? The pasta and sauce are baked in a frying pan, which saves on washing up and involves fewer steps. This summery and super creamy variation takes a little time to prepare, but it's absolutely delicious.

Serves 4 to 6
Prep time: 20 minutes
Cooking time: 1 hour and 20 minutes

1 kg ripe tomatoes, not too large
3 tbsp olive oil
1 clove garlic
½ tsp raw cane sugar
2 tsp herbes de Provence
Salt, pepper

1 bowl of white bean béchamel (see recipe p. 33)

10 lasagne sheets
1 tbsp sunflower seeds
A few fresh basil leaves

Preheat the oven to 180°C (gas mark 4).

Peel, degerm and finely chop the garlic. Wash the tomatoes, cut them in half and place in a cast-iron frying pan cut side up, pressing them together tightly and overlapping them. Sprinkle with the garlic, sugar and 1 teaspoon of the herbs de Provence, add salt and pepper and drizzle with 2 tablespoons of olive oil. Put the frying pan on a rack in the oven and cook for about 1 hour, or until the tomatoes are very soft. You can press on them lightly so they release some juice.

In the meantime, prepare the béchamel sauce and break the lasagne sheets into different-sized pieces.

Take the frying pan out of the oven, insert the lasagne sheets between the layers of tomato and pour the béchamel sauce over everything. Drizzle with the remaining olive oil and add a little more herbs de Provence and the sunflower seeds.

Increase the oven temperature to 200°C (gas mark 6) and put the lasagne in the oven for about 20 minutes. The sauce should be creamy and the lasagne sheets tender. Top with a few fresh basil leaves and serve immediately.

Spaghetti bolognese

The secrets of my spaghetti bolognese are a good tomato passata, a long cooking time and textured soy protein that works wonders in all dishes that call for minced meat. Freeze the extra sauce in silicone muffin tins for when you crave a little something.

Serves 4
Prep time: 15 minutes
Cooking time: About 2 hours
Resting time: 20 minutes

- 1 litre vegetable stock of your choice
- 200 g fine textured soy protein (TSP)
- 1 tbsp dried mushrooms (optional)
- 2 yellow onions
- 1 clove garlic
- 1 carrot
- 2 tbsp olive oil
- 150 ml red wine
- 150 ml plant-based milk (almond, soya, oat)
- 2 tbsp tomato paste
- 600 g passata
- 3-4 sprigs of thyme
- 2 bay leaves
- 1 large pinch of caster sugar
- Salt, pepper
- 400 g spaghetti (or other pasta of your choice)

Very finely chop the peeled onions, the peeled and degermed garlic and the carrot. Sauté in olive oil in a cast-iron casserole or heavy-bottomed saucepan for 3 minutes. Add the drained TSP and cook for another 2 minutes, stirring regularly. Add the wine and milk as well as the tomato paste, mix well then add the passata, thyme, bay leaves and sugar. Add salt and pepper, stir, cover partially to avoid splatters and leave to cook for about 2 hours (an hour and a half at the very least), over a very low heat, stirring occasionally. After this time, cook the spaghetti, drain and combine with the bolognese sauce. If you like, sprinkle with plant-based Parmesan or toasted sunflower seeds (see the topping recipes in the introduction).

Tip

Put the TSP into a bowl, cover with hot stock and leave to rehydrate for about 20 minutes. If you wish, you can add the chopped mushrooms together with the stock.

Conchigliette and caramelised shallots gratin

This simple dish, which evokes childhood memories, is a great way to use up leftover pasta (about 700 g of cooked pasta). The combination of firm and silken tofu gives the dish a creamy yet satisfying texture, while the caramelised shallots make it totally irresistible. Pair it with a nice crisp salad for a complete, protein-packed meal, and don't forget that it reheats beautifully the next day.

Serves 4 to 6
Prep time: 30 minutes
Cooking time: 30 minutes

8 shallots
2 tbsp olive oil
2 pinches of brown caster sugar
1 pinch of fleur de sel
300 g conchigliette (regular or semi-wholegrain pasta)
300 g silken tofu
150 g firm tofu
1 heaped tsp mustard
Salt, pepper

Peel and finely chop the shallots and sauté in olive oil in a small pan for 2 to 3 minutes. Add the sugar and salt. Mix, cover and leave to caramelise over a very low heat for about 10 minutes. Set aside.

Preheat the oven to 180°C (gas mark 4).

To cook the pasta, follow the instructions on the packet. Drain and tip into a large bowl. In the meantime, mix the silken tofu with the mustard and season with salt and pepper. Coarsely mash the firm tofu with a fork; don't over mash as the texture should be irregular. Mix the silken tofu cream with the firm tofu and shallots, then with the pasta. Transfer to a casserole dish or individual ramekins and bake for 20 minutes. Serve immediately.

Fettuccine Alfredo

This 100% plant-based variation of the famous Italian recipe is just as creamy but much lighter than the original, and it holds a little secret: cauliflower roasted with smoked paprika and cashew nuts for an amazing 'cheesy' flavour and lots of creaminess. Serve with grilled mushrooms or baby spinach, for example.

Serves 4
Prep time: 15 minutes
Cooking time: 40 minutes
Resting time: 4 hours

1 small cauliflower
1½ tbsp olive oil
2 tsp smoked paprika (optional)
100 g cashew nuts (soaked for about 4 hours)
200 ml oat or soya milk
2 heaped tbsp malted yeast
1 tsp apple cider vinegar
1 scant tsp onion granules
2 pinches of garlic powder (or 2 cloves of garlic)
400 g fettuccine
Salt, pepper

Soak the cashew nuts in a large bowl of cold water for 3 to 4 hours.

Wash the cauliflower, dry it gently and remove the stem. Cut it vertically into large 1.5-cm thick slices. Arrange them in a single layer in a large baking dish, or on a baking sheet lined with greaseproof paper. Mix the olive oil with the paprika and drizzle over the cauliflower.

Season with salt and pepper and bake for about 30 minutes at 180°C (gas mark 4), or until the cauliflower is tender all the way through.

Leave to cool for a few minutes, then blend 200 grams of roasted cauliflower (save the rest for another use, see Tip) with the rinsed and drained cashew nuts, plant-based milk, malted yeast, vinegar, garlic and onion, salt and pepper, until smooth and creamy.

To cook the fettuccine, follow the instructions on the packet. Drain and mix with ⅔ of the Alfredo sauce. Serve the pasta hot with the remaining sauce separately and with plant-based Parmesan.

Tip

Chances are you might have some leftover cauliflower. Serve it warm as an appetiser, blend it with boiled potatoes and stock for a delicious velouté soup or to top whatever pasta you feel like. It'll keep in the fridge for 48 hours in an airtight container.

Mushroom risoni risotto

Risoni (meaning 'big rice' in Italian), also known as orzo, is a small pasta shaped like a grain of rice, often cooked in a soup or to make risotto. This is a simple, creamy and al dente version, made with shallots and button mushrooms. You can use any small mushrooms you like. Enhance this recipe with a good spoonful of malted yeast and replace the risoni with other small pasta (crozets, alphabet pasta, etc.).

Serves 4
Prep time: 15 minutes
Cooking time: 30 minutes

2 tsp vegetable stock powder
2 shallots
4 tbsp olive oil
300 g risoni (or other small pasta)
500 g button mushrooms
100 ml plant-based cream
1 tbsp finely chopped parsley
Salt, pepper

Prepare the stock by mixing the vegetable stock powder with 750 ml of water, heat to a simmer and keep it warm. Clean and finely chop the mushrooms, then fry for 10 minutes in a frying pan with half of the olive oil. Season with salt and pepper and set aside.

Peel and slice the shallots and brown them in a large saucepan with the remaining olive oil. Add the risoni and fry for 5 minutes, stirring regularly. Add 1 ladleful of stock and cook at a simmer, stirring often. When the stock has almost all been absorbed, add a little more stock and continue in this way until there's no more stock and the pasta is just al dente (about 12 minutes). Stir in the cream, then the mushrooms and parsley. Serve immediately.

Fried noodles al'arrabiata

Pasta 'al'arrabiata' is a recipe from Rome made with garlic, chilli and tomatoes, traditionally made with penne rigate. I've borrowed from Asian cuisine by replacing the latter with noodles (my favourites are made from brown rice, but you can also use white rice or wheat noodles) and sautéed everything quickly in a wok instead of letting the tomatoes cook slowly. I've also added some diced lacto-fermented tofu, which adds the missing freshness to this rather fiery recipe – I particularly like the tamari one, but plain tofu works well too. Serve it immediately because noodles dry out quickly, especially rice ones.

Serves 4
Prep time: 15 minutes
Cooking time: 10 minutes

- 200 g lacto-fermented tofu (plain or with tamari)
- 2 cloves garlic
- 1 red pepper (or 2, if you love peppers)
- 3 tbsp olive oil
- 5 ripe but firm tomatoes
- 1 pinch of raw cane sugar
- 350 g Asian noodles (rice, wheat)
- 2 tbsp finely chopped parsley

Bring a generous amount of water to the boil in a saucepan. In the meantime, cut the tofu into small 1-cm cubes (no bigger) and set aside.

Peel, degerm and finely chop the garlic, cut the chilli into fine slices (remove the seeds if you wish). Wash and dice the tomatoes.

When the water boils, tip in the pasta.

Heat the oil in a frying pan or wok, add the garlic and chilli and cook for a few moments, until fragrant. Add the tomatoes and sugar and sauté for about 5 minutes or until the tomatoes disintegrate. When the pasta is cooked, drain and tip it over the tomato mixture. Add the parsley and tofu, mix gently and cook for another minute, then serve immediately.

Spaghetti carbonara with aubergine 'bacon'

Carbonara is something of a nutritional heresy as it's made with cream, eggs, cheese and bacon. Fortunately, there are more judicious, yet equally tasty versions, such as this recipe made with aubergine bacon and slow-cooked shallots.

Serves 4
Prep time: 30 minutes
Cooking time: 40 minutes

- 2 large aubergines
- 2 tsp onion granules
- 1 level tsp garlic powder
- 30 ml tamari
- 1 tsp maple syrup
- 1 pinch of chilli seasoning (optional)
- 80 ml olive oil plus 2 tbsp
- 6 shallots
- 1 generous pinch of brown caster sugar
- 1 quantity of cashew nut cream (see recipe p. 28. Remember to soak the nuts for a few hours)
- 500 g spaghetti
- 1 handful of basil leaves (optional)
- Salt

Preheat the oven to 120°C (gas mark 1).

Combine the onion granules, garlic powder, tamari, maple syrup, chilli if using, ½ teaspoon of salt and olive oil in a bowl. Wash the aubergines, then quarter them lengthways and cut into very fine strips (maximum 1 mm thick) using a mandoline or vegetable peeler. Arrange them without overlapping on a baking tray lined with greaseproof paper (you can do this in two stages, or on two different trays). Brush them with the mixture, then gently turn them over and do the same on the other side. Bake, one sheet at a time, for 25 to 30 minutes, or until the aubergine slices are golden and crisp around the edges. Remove from the oven and leave to cool.

Meanwhile, fry the finely chopped peeled shallots in a small saucepan with 2 tablespoons of olive oil, the sugar and a generous pinch of salt for 2 to 3 minutes, stirring. Cover and leave to simmer for 10 minutes. To cook the pasta, follow the instructions on the packet. Drain, keeping a little of the cooking water and mix it and the pasta with the cashew nut cream and shallots. Serve very hot with the aubergine bacon and a few basil leaves.

Trofiette al ragù

Pasta al ragù is a speciality of Bologna that's traditionally made with tagliatelle and has given its name to the world-famous spaghetti Bolognese. I've replaced the meat with lentils, and although the cooking time is a little shorter than that of the original recipe, the result is equally delicious: meltingly tender, fragrant and silky thanks to the soffritto – minced vegetables cooked gently in olive oil until reduced.

Serves 4
Prep time: 20 minutes
Cooking time: 1 hour 10 minutes

1 yellow onion
1 small clove garlic
1 medium carrot
1 small rib of celery
4 tbsp olive oil
180 g green lentils
1 tsp vegetable stock powder
1 piece of kombu seaweed
2 tbsp tomato paste
100 ml red wine
300 g trofiette or tagliatelle
Salt, pepper

Peel and mince the onion, garlic, carrot and celery. Put them in a cast-iron casserole or thick-bottomed frying pan and cook over a low heat in the olive oil for about 20 minutes, stirring occasionally (add a little more oil if necessary).

Meanwhile, cook the lentils: rinse them quickly, put them in a large cast-iron casserole and cover with cold water. Bring to the boil, discard the cooking water, return the lentils to the casserole and cover with a generous amount of cold water, the vegetable stock and kombu seaweed. Boil again and cook until the lentils are cooked but still firm (about 20 minutes). Drain, keeping 100 ml of the cooking water.

Add the tomato paste to the casserole and cook for another 5 minutes, stirring, then add the drained lentils. Season with salt and pepper, cook for 5 minutes over a medium heat, add the red wine and the reserved stock, and leave to simmer for about 20 minutes, until the mixture is creamy.

To cook the pasta, follow the instructions on the packet. Drain, reserving a few tablespoons of cooking water. Mix the water into the lentils, then pour over the pasta, stir quickly and serve immediately.

Autumn minestrone, cauliflower, chestnuts and Jerusalem artichokes

> *This simple and nutritious peasant dish is traditionally made with tomatoes and seasonal vegetables and enhanced with pasta and dried beans. This autumnal version combines Jerusalem artichokes with cauliflower, chestnuts and thyme for a beautiful burst of flavours and lots of originality.*

Serves 6 to 8
Prep time: 15 minutes
Cooking time: 35 minutes

- 130 g cooked white beans (or 60 g dried beans)
- 2 shallots
- 2 tbsp olive oil
- 2 heaped tsp vegetable stock powder
- 3 sprigs of fresh thyme or 1 tsp dried thyme
- 1 tbsp tamari
- 1 small cauliflower (about 600 g)
- 300 g Jerusalem artichokes
- 180 g small pasta of your choice
- 150 g cooked chestnuts (plain, with no other added ingredients)
- Salt, pepper

If you're using dry beans, cook them in a generous amount of boiling water until just tender (about 30 minutes). Remember to soak them overnight in cold water and then rinse well. If they're canned, rinse and drain them. Set aside.

Add vegetable stock powder to 1.5 litres of water and bring to the boil with the thyme and tamari.

Wash the cauliflower and cut into florets. Brush the Jerusalem artichokes and cut into thin strips about 2 mm thick.

Sweat the peeled and finely chopped shallots in a cast-iron casserole with the oil for 2 to 3 minutes. Add the vegetables and fry for 5 minutes, stirring occasionally. Add the stock (the vegetables should be well covered), stir and simmer for 10 minutes. Add the pasta, cook for 10 minutes, then finish with the chestnuts and white beans.

Season generously with salt and pepper, stir gently and cook for another 5 minutes. Taste, adjust the seasoning if necessary and serve hot.

Tip

Jerusalem artichokes keep very well as long as they're not washed – simply store them in your fridge's crisper drawer. Here's an original idea for using this root vegetable: try a carpaccio, cut them, raw, into thin strips and drizzled with hazelnut oil, a dash of orange juice and a generous pinch of fleur de sel. Great as an appetiser or as a snack.

Healthy Pasta Packed With Vitamins

Courgetti, roasted garlic and smoked paprika

Deliciously crunchy and wonderfully colourful, this totally veggie recipe is just as good as an appetiser or as a side dish for a main course of grains or with a beautiful vegetable bruschetta. Adding slices of avocado, corn kernels and/ or diced tofu make a more filling dish that you can enjoy as a main course. It's best to use a wok or a metal pan as they conduct heat well, allowing you to sauté the vegetables quickly without them drowning in their own juices. Serve immediately, while they're lovely and crunchy.

Serves 4
Prep time: 15 minutes
Cooking time: 20 minutes

6 courgettes (approx. 1.2 kg)
1 large head of garlic
5 tbsp olive oil
1 tbsp lemon juice
2 tsp smoked paprika
Salt, pepper

Detach the garlic cloves without peeling them and place in a small ovenproof dish. Drizzle with 2 tablespoons of olive oil and cook for about 20 minutes at 210°C (gas mark 6-7). Leave to cool.

Prepare the courgetti: wash the courgettes and cut them into spaghetti (see p. 20). Heat 2 tablespoons of olive oil in a wok or the same sort of pan, put in the courgetti, season with salt and pepper and stir-fry for a minute and a half, then leave to soften for 3 minutes off the heat.

In the meantime, peel the garlic cloves, mash 6 of them with a fork with the lemon juice, smoked paprika and the remaining olive oil, mixing until fairly smooth. Gently stir into the courgetti.

Serve immediately with the remaining garlic and, if you wish, toasted sunflower seeds and/or a few fresh basil leaves.

Mafaldine pasta with sage, fresh broad beans and crunchy almonds

There's no butter in this recipe, so it's a bit of a departure from the classic sage and butter pasta dish, but the olive oil is deliciously flavoured with sage, garlic and lemon, crunchy toasted almonds and fresh beans, which you can also find frozen all year round. Feel free to add whole sage leaves to the pan, they're very decorative and deliciously crispy.

Serves 4
Prep time: 15 minutes
Cooking time: 10 minutes

160 g shelled and peeled beans (fresh or frozen)
30 g unpeeled almonds
400 g mafaldine or other pasta of your choice
60 ml olive oil
2 cloves garlic
10 large sage leaves
Zest of ½ a lemon
Salt, pepper

Bring a generous amount of water to a boil for the pasta and a smaller one for the beans.

Dry roast the almonds for a few minutes in a frying pan until golden, crunchy and fragrant. Set aside.

Cook the beans for 3 minutes (if frozen) or 1 minute (if fresh) in boiling salted water, then drain, run under cold water and set aside.

To cook the pasta, follow the instructions on the packet.

In the meantime, heat the olive oil in a frying pan and add the peeled, degermed and chopped garlic, and brown for 1 minute. Add the chopped sage leaves and cook for a further 3 to 4 minutes, then add the beans and lemon zest and cook for another minute while stirring. Season with salt and pepper.

Drain the pasta, tip it into a dish and add the sage mixture and the almonds. Serve immediately with a little plant-based Parmesan (see recipe p. 24).

Farfalle with wild garlic pesto, hemp and baby radishes

This pasta is enhanced with a delicious spring pesto that's packed with vitamins and nutrients thanks to the combination of hemp seeds and wild garlic. As it keeps for a month in the fridge, you can benefit from the properties of wild garlic long after the season has ended.

Serves 4
Prep time: 10 minutes
Soaking time: 3-4 hours
Cooking time: 10 minutes

For the pesto
60 g cashew nuts, soaked for 3 to 4 hours in a generous amount of cold water
1 bunch of wild garlic (about 50 g)
2 heaped tbsp hemp seeds
½ organic lemon
60–100 ml olive oil or rapeseed oil (or a mixture of both)
Fleur de sel
Ground pepper

500 g farfalle (or other medium-sized pasta)
10 baby radishes

Prepare the pesto: rinse and drain the cashew nuts. Wash and gently dry the bunch of wild garlic, cut off the ends of the stems. Blend the cashew nuts, hemp seeds, lemon zest, salt and 30 ml of oil in small batches to the desired consistency. Add another 30 ml of oil and blend again. Taste and add a little salt, freshly ground pepper or oil if you wish. Pour into an airtight jar and store in the fridge, covering with a little oil to stop surface drying.

To cook the pasta, follow the instructions on the packet. Drain and mix in a dash of olive oil and the lemon zest and juice. Stir in the pesto and some finely sliced radishes and their tops if they're fresh. Serve immediately, or leave to cool and enjoy as a salad.

Leftover pesto?

Use it in a sandwich or as a crêpe stuffing, with a bowl of rice or in a spring pasta dish; it's delicious with multi-coloured tagliatelle or mixed with béchamel sauce in a spring vegetable lasagne.

All raw lasagne

If raw food tickles your taste buds, try this beautiful lasagne: crunchy courgette slices, melted okara cheese, sun-dried tomato sauce and hemp avocado pesto, all topped with basil and sunflower seeds. It packs a vitamin punch.

Serves 3 to 4
Prep time: 30 minutes
Soaking time: 4 hours

For the okara cheese:
100 g okara (almonds, cashew nuts, etc.)
3 tsp lemon juice
1 tsp apple cider vinegar
1 small clove garlic
2 tbsp olive oil
1 small shallot, peeled and chopped
2 tbsp malted yeast
Salt, pepper
A few spoonfuls of plant-based milk (optional)

For the tomato sauce:
50 g sun-dried tomatoes (soaked for at least 2 hours in a little water)
1 clove garlic
3 fresh tomatoes, not too juicy (about 250 g)
1 soft medjool date
1 tsp lemon juice
1 tbsp olive oil
2 tsp herbes de Provence
Salt

For the avocado pesto:
250 g avocado flesh (about 3 small avocados)
15 basil leaves
5 tbsp hemp seeds (or cashew nuts soaked for 4 hours in a generous amount of cold water, then rinsed and drained)
Juice of ½ a lemon
Salt, pepper

2 long courgettes (or 4 small round ones)
Basil, sunflower seeds, olive oil and fleur de sel (optional)

Prepare the okara cheese: mix the peeled, degermed and crushed garlic, the shallot and the other ingredients until smooth but not liquid (add a few spoonfuls of plant-based milk if necessary). Press into a bowl or ramekin and set aside in the fridge.

Prepare the tomato sauce: blend the dried tomatoes (without their soaking water) with the fresh tomatoes cut into pieces, the peeled, degermed and crushed clove of garlic, the pitted date, the lemon juice, olive oil and herbes de Provence, and add a little salt. Set aside in the fridge.

Prepare the avocado pesto: blend the avocado flesh with the basil leaves, hemp (or cashew nuts) and lemon juice. Season with salt and pepper.

Cut the courgettes lengthwise into slices no thicker than 2 mm, then divide them in half. On each plate place a slice of courgette, some plant-based cheese, a slice of courgette, some avocado pesto, a slice of courgette, some tomato sauce and another slice of courgette. Decorate with basil leaves or toasted sunflower seeds and a drizzle of olive oil.

Recycling

If you have any leftover tomato sauce, add it to courgetti sautéed with garlic: quick and delicious.

Trofiette, poivrade artichokes, rocket and sunflower 'pine nuts'

These pretty trofiette are enhanced with small artichokes sprinkled with herbs, toasted sunflower seeds (a lot less expensive than pine nuts) and piquant rocket leaves. You can also make this dish with penne rigate or spaghetti.

Serves 4
Prep time: 15 minutes
Cooking time: 30 minutes

10 poivrade artichokes
1 lemon
4 tbsp olive oil
2 cloves garlic
150 ml dry white wine
1 tsp dried thyme
500 g trofiette (or another pasta of your choice)
2 handfuls of rocket leaves
2 tbsp sunflower seeds
Salt, pepper

Prepare the artichokes: remove the hardest outer leaves, then cut off the stem and top third of the artichokes. Cut the remaining part into quarters and sprinkle with half of the lemon juice. Heat 2 tablespoons of oil in a frying pan, put in the artichoke pieces and fry for 3 to 4 minutes. Add the peeled, degermed and minced garlic, the white wine and thyme. Season with salt and pepper, lower the heat and cook for 20 to 25 minutes, until the artichokes are tender (you can add a little more water or wine during cooking if necessary).

Meanwhile, bring a generous amount of water to the boil.

To cook the pasta, follow the instructions on the packet. Drain the pasta, reserving a little of the cooking water, mix it with the remaining olive oil and lemon juice and pour it over the pasta, add salt and mix well. Add the artichokes and rocket and mix gently. Dry roast the sunflower seeds for a few minutes in a frying pan, stirring regularly until just golden. Sprinkle them over the pasta and serve immediately.

Comment

These small poivrade artichokes are also called 'violets de Provence' thanks to their pretty purple colour tinged with light green. They're particularly tender and, because they aren't fully grown they have no choke. To prepare them, simply remove the base and the hardest outer leaves.

One pot 'cheesy broccoli' pasta

Never heard of one pot pasta? This is a super simple but brilliant idea: combine the pasta with all the ingredients for the sauce in a large saucepan, add a little water, cover and let it do the job. In barely more than 10 minutes you've got a creamy fragrant dish... and only one pan to wash. This is my cheesy broccoli version, pairing cashew nut butter and malted yeast pasta with crunchy little broccoli. Make it with whatever little green vegetables you like.

Serves 4
Prep time: 15 minutes
Cooking time: 10 minutes

- 1 large head of broccoli (about 500 g)
- 2 shallots
- 2 tbsp olive oil
- 300 g medium-sized pasta (lumache, penne, fusilli, rotini, etc.)
- 2 level tsp vegetable stock powder (or 1 crumbled cube)
- 1 tsp granulated or powdered garlic
- 4 tbsp malted yeast (or more if you wish)
- 1 heaped tsp mustard
- 1 tsp dried thyme
- 50 g cashew nut butter
- Salt, pepper

Cut off the broccoli florets and wash them, peel the stalk and cut it into slices. Set aside.

Brown the peeled and chopped shallots in the olive oil in a large saucepan for 3 minutes, stirring. Add the pasta, the stock, garlic, yeast, mustard, thyme and cashew nut butter and 850 ml of water. Mix well, cover tightly and leave to simmer for about 10 minutes, or the time indicated on the packet, adding the broccoli 4 minutes before the end (or before if you like it soft). Season with salt and pepper. Serve immediately with plant-based Parmesan if you wish (see recipe p. 24).

Torsade, roasted pepper cream and basil

This summery recipe combines roasted peppers and a balsamic-vinegar-scented white almond butter in a smooth and very flavoursome creamy sauce. Try it with rotini, fusilli or penne, but also with courgetti.

Serves 4
Prep time: 15 minutes
Cooking time: 30 minutes
Resting time: 1 hour

3 large red peppers
2 cloves garlic
3 tbsp balsamic vinegar
40 g white almond butter
2 tsp lemon juice
1 pinch Espelette pepper
400 g torsade
1 bunch of basil leaves
Salt, pepper
2 tbsp sunflower seeds (optional)

Wash the peppers and place them whole on a baking tray lined with greaseproof paper or in a large ovenproof dish with the garlic. Cook under the grill, turning occasionally, until black blisters appear all over. Set aside the garlic. Put the peppers into an airtight bag, close it and leave for about 1 hour. Then skin them and remove the seeds and the white ribs (you can place them under cold running water to speed up the process). Put them in the bowl of a food processor with the garlic, the vinegar, almond butter, lemon juice and Espelette pepper. Season with salt and pepper and process until smooth.

To cook the pasta, follow the instructions on the packet. Drain and return it to the saucepan. Add the creamy pepper sauce and mix (it'll warm up when it comes into contact with the pasta, but you can also heat it for a few moments over a low heat). Serve with fresh basil and sunflower seeds dry roasted for a few minutes in a frying pan.

Tip

If you have any leftover pepper sauce, spread it on bruschetta or pizza, with olives and plant-based cheese.

Mung bean, avocado and lime orecchiette salad

This great, nutritious cold salad can be made ahead of time and kept in the fridge for up to 24 hours – perfect for a picnic. Don't add the avocados until the last minute (they blacken quickly). If you wish, you can replace the mung beans with other beans or lentils.

Serves 6

Soaking time: Overnight
Prep time: 20 minutes
Cooking time: 30 minutes

100 g mung beans, soaked overnight in a generous amount of water
500 g orecchiette pasta
3 ripe avocados
1 clove garlic
Juice of ½ a lemon
Juice of 2 limes
2 tbsp sesame oil
1 tbsp olive oil
2 tsp tamari
1 bunch of fresh coriander
Sea salt

Rinse the mung beans for a long time under cold running water. Put them in a saucepan, cover with a generous amount of cold water and simmer for 15 to 20 minutes with a pinch of salt: when done they should still be a little firm. Drain and set aside.

To cook the orecchiette, follow the instructions on the packet.

Meanwhile, prepare the dressing: crush the peeled and degermed garlic clove and add the lemon and lime juice, the vegetable oils and tamari.

Drain the pasta, refresh under cold water and transfer to a large bowl. Add the mung beans and the dressing and mix gently.

Season with a little salt. Garnish with sliced avocado and chopped coriander. Serve cold.

Tip

Unbelievable but true: the best way to extend the life of an avocado once cut open, at least to my knowledge, is to keep the stone in cold water while the avocado is in the fridge. Try it, you'll be amazed.

Sweet potato spaghetti with caramelised orange

This simple recipe brings me joy in winter when I've got a craving for sweet potatoes, but don't want to wait 40 minutes for it to cook in the oven. Here, it takes only 5 minutes to make delicious veggie spaghetti, tender and lightly caramelised with orange. Enhanced with red onion and fresh coriander, it's one of my favourite combinations, but you can add any herbs you like and/or a handful of pecans for crunch. Serve immediately before they get too soft.

Serves 2
Prep time: 8 minutes
Cooking time: 5 minutes

- 1 large sweet potato
- 1 small red onion
- 1 clove garlic
- 1 tbsp coconut oil
- 2 pinches of chilli flakes
- Juice of ½ orange
- 3 sprigs of fresh thyme
- 1 tbsp finely chopped fresh coriander
- Salt, pepper

Scrub the sweet potato, peel it if you wish and cut it into spaghetti. (See p.20)

Peel and slice the red onion into thin rings. Peel, degerm and crush the garlic. Heat the coconut oil in a wok or frying pan, add the garlic and chilli, stir-fry for 1 minute, then add the onion and sweet potato spaghetti. Cook for a further 2 to 3 minutes, stirring often. Add the orange juice and thyme, lower the heat, cover and cook for 3 to 4 minutes, taking a look from time to time: the spaghetti should be cooked but still firm. Season with salt and pepper, take off the heat and serve immediately with chopped fresh coriander.

Linguine with kale and pumpkin seed pesto

This pesto made with kale – a kind of cabbage with lots of health benefits – also contains toasted pumpkin seeds, almonds and a touch of malted yeast, as well as olive and rapeseed oils for a perfect balance of essential fatty acids. Enjoy as a hot or cold pasta dish, as an appetiser or spread on bruschetta.

Serves 4
Prep time: 15 minutes
Cooking time: 10 minutes

200 g crisp kale leaves
50 g pumpkin seeds
50 g almonds
1 clove garlic
2 tbsp lemon juice
1-2 tbsp malted yeast (or more if you wish)
1 tsp salt
40 ml olive oil
40 ml rapeseed oil
500 g linguine (or other pasta of your choice)

Wash the kale leaves, detach the leafy parts from the stems and dry with a clean tea towel. Dry roast the pumpkin seeds for a few minutes in a frying pan until they pop, but don't let them burn. Put them in the jar of a blender with the kale, almonds, peeled and degermed garlic clove, lemon juice, malted yeast and salt. Use the pulse button to blend to the desired texture, then add the oils little by little while blending. Increase the amount of oil if it's too dry for your taste. Store in a jar, adding a little oil after each use.

To cook the linguine, follow the instructions on the packet. Drain and toss with about half of the jar of kale pesto and serve immediately, sprinkling a few toasted pumpkin seeds as a topping if you like.

Variations

Replace the almonds with cashew nuts for a more melt-in-your-mouth texture; increase the quantity of oil or try making it with other kinds – hazelnut oil is delicious with kale, while hemp oil will give a boost to the flavour of this green veggie.

Conchigliette, slow-cooked fennel, pomegranate and baby leaf spinach

This pretty and colourful dish highlights a vegetable that's rarely associated with pasta: fennel. Here, it's gently slow cooked with thyme and a few slices of apple before being paired with pomegranate seeds and crisp spinach leaves for a great conchigliette dish. It's the perfect recipe for when it's still winter but you can't wait for spring to arrive. Swap the pomegranate seeds for dried cranberries and the conchigliette with other small-sized pasta (farfalle, lumache, small penne, rotini, etc..)

Serves 4
Prep time: 15 minutes
Cooking time: 30 minutes

2 fennel bulbs
1 small apple
4 tbsp olive oil
1 tsp raw cane sugar
1 tsp dried thyme
2 pinches fleur de sel
400 g conchigliette or other pasta of the same size
1 pomegranate
2 bunches of baby leaf spinach
Juice of ½ a lemon
Salt, pepper

Wash the fennel, remove the sprigs (keep the fronds) and the outer layer if it's leathery, slice the rest into 3-mm slices. Cut the apple into quarters, then into slices. Sauté the fennel and apple with 2 scant tablespoons of olive oil in a cast-iron casserole or heavy-bottomed saucepan for 3 minutes. Add the sugar, thyme and fleur de sel, cover and leave to cook for 15 to 20 minutes over a very low heat: the fennel should be tender and slightly caramelised. Set aside.

To cook the pasta, follow the instructions on the packet. Meanwhile, remove the seeds from the pomegranate and wash the spinach.

Drain the pasta and toss with the remaining olive oil and lemon juice, season with salt and pepper. Add two thirds of the fennel, pomegranate and spinach, mix very gently and add the remaining toppings and the reserved fennel fronds. Serve immediately, or keep refrigerated to enjoy this pasta dish cold.

Shirataki express, red onion, fresh coriander and peanuts

I immediately fell in love with these fine noodles made from konjac. They're very firm with a totally neutral flavour – all you have to do is cook them for 2 minutes in boiling water before serving them as you like, hot or cold in a salad. This is my 'fusion' version, to which you can add slices of avocado or cubes of tofu for a complete but light meal.

Serves 1
Prep time: 5 minutes
Cooking time: 2 minutes

- 1 packet shirataki (about 150 g)
- 1 tsp tamari or shoyu
- 1 tsp rice wine vinegar
- 2 tsp sesame oil (plain or toasted)
- ½ red onion
- 1 heaped tbsp peanuts
- 1 scant tbsp fresh coriander, chopped

Rinse the shirataki thoroughly in a large colander under cold water, then cook for 2 minutes in boiling water. Drain thoroughly before transferring to a large bowl. Mix the tamari, vinegar and sesame oil, pour over the shirataki and stir.

Peel and chop the onion as finely as possible (preferably use a mandoline) and add to the bowl along with the fresh coriander and coarsely chopped peanuts. Serve immediately or leave to cool slightly*.

Comment

Shirataki can be found in packets for one person in Asian grocery shops and in some organic food shops.

*To serve this dish as a salad, run the shirataki under cold water before mixing with the dressing.

Tri-coloured tagliatelle, vegetables and white miso cream sauce

This simple carrot and courgette tagliatelle recipe is enhanced with a creamy cashew nut and white miso sauce that's packed with digestive enzymes. If you can find unpasteurised miso, go for it – it's so much better.

Serves 4
Prep time: 20 minutes
Cooking time: 10 minutes

Miso cream
50 g white miso
20 g cashew nut butter
40 ml sesame oil
20 ml olive oil
1 tbsp cider vinegar
1 tsp tamari
Salt, pepper

2 large carrots
2 long courgettes
400 g wheat or rice tagliatelle
Fresh coriander, gomasio (optional)

Prepare the creamy miso sauce: put the miso, cashew nut butter, oils and tamari in a small blender and blend until smooth and creamy. Season with salt and pepper, a little tamari or cider vinegar to taste. Set aside.

To cook the pasta, follow the instructions on the packet.

Meanwhile, wash or scrub the carrots and courgettes, then make tagliatelle (see p. 20). Bring 1 cm of water to the boil in a saucepan. Put in the vegetables, cover and cook for 1 minute over a medium heat, then leave to soften for 5 minutes off the heat without removing the lid.

When the pasta is cooked, drain it, keeping a small amount of the cooking water, mix it with the miso sauce, pour it over the pasta and stir. Add the drained vegetables and mix very gently. Serve immediately, with fresh coriander and/or gomasio if you wish.

Inspirations From Around the World

Ramen, caramelised tempeh and orange-glazed carrots

A veritable institution in Japan, ramen is a stock enriched with wheat noodles and your choice of toppings. This is my favourite version with carrots baked in an orange, garlic and ginger marinade, and teriyaki tempeh, caramelised with tamari and maple syrup.

Serves 2
Prep time: 30 minutes
Cooking time: 40 minutes

For the carrots:
300 g carrots
1 small clove garlic
1 cm piece fresh ginger
Juice of ½ an orange
2 tbsp olive oil
1 tsp maple syrup
Salt, pepper

For the caramelised tempeh:
100 g tempeh
1 tbsp olive or coconut oil
2 tbsp tamari or shoyu
1 tbsp coconut nectar

For the stock:
1 heaped tsp vegetable stock powder
2 tsp tamari
2 tsp miso of your choice (rice, barley, 100% soy)

160 g ramen (or soba) noodles
1 tbsp finely chopped fresh coriander
1 heaped tsp white sesame seeds

Preheat the oven to 180°C (gas mark 4).

Scrub the carrots, cut them in half or quarters lengthwise and arrange them in a single layer in an ovenproof dish or on a baking tray lined with greaseproof paper.

In a small bowl, combine the peeled, degermed and crushed garlic, peeled and grated ginger, orange juice, olive oil and maple syrup. Drizzle it over the carrots, season with salt and pepper and bake for about 40 minutes, or until the carrots are soft, turning them halfway through the cooking time. Turn off the oven and leave them there.

Cut the tempeh into small slices and fry in hot oil until golden. Mix the tamari, coconut nectar and 3 teaspoons of cold water and pour over the tempeh. Let it caramelise over a low heat on both sides until golden brown and the liquid has evaporated.

Prepare the stock with 500 ml of water, the vegetable stock powder and the tamari. When it's hot, add the miso off the heat, whisk to mix well and cover to keep it warm.

To cook the noodles, follow the instructions on the packet, then drain. Divide them between two bowls, add the carrots and tempeh and pour in the stock. Garnish with coriander and sesame seeds and serve immediately.

One pot coco-curry pasta

Simple and quick to prepare, this novel one-pot pasta recipe has an Asian feel thanks to the addition of coconut milk, cashew butter and yellow curry. Yellow curry or Bombay curry, that's very mild and fragrant– made from 70 different spices – is ideal for the whole family, including children. If you like stronger flavours, use a spicier curry mix. If you have curry paste, so much the better; if using paste, add it at the beginning of the recipe, when you sauté the garlic and ginger. In the off-season, swap the courgettes for diced carrots or squash, chopped leeks or a mix of green veggies (peas, shelled beans, halved green beans, etc.).

Serves 4
Prep time: 10 minutes
Cooking time: 12 minutes

- 1 small yellow onion
- 1 tbsp olive or coconut oil
- 1 clove garlic
- 1 cm piece fresh ginger
- 3 tsp yellow curry powder (or 1 tbsp yellow curry paste)
- 200 ml canned coconut milk
- 350 ml vegetable stock
- 300 g penne, rigate or macaroni
- 300 g courgette or other seasonal vegetables
- 1 tbsp cashew butter
- Salt, pepper

Sauté the peeled and sliced onion in the oil for 3 minutes in a cast-iron casserole or heavy-bottomed saucepan. Add the peeled, degermed and chopped garlic and the peeled and chopped ginger (the curry paste, if using) and sauté for another minute.

Add the curry powder, coconut milk and stock, then the pasta, diced courgettes and the cashew butter, season with salt and pepper and mix well.

Cover and simmer for 10 to 12 minutes, stirring gently three or four times. If necessary, add a little more coconut milk or stock and cook a little longer: the pasta should be cooked and the sauce creamy. Serve immediately.

Savoyard gratin, crozets, leeks and smoked tofu 'lardons'

This 100% alpine dish (or almost) is a gourmet variation of the famous crozet gratin made with Reblochon cheese. Here, I use a smooth 'cheese' sauce made with malted yeast and my little extra touch: slightly caramelised leeks. Of course, like any self-respecting gratin, this one is even better reheated the next day.

Serves 4
Prep time: 25 minutes
Cooking time: 35 minutes

300 g crozets
2 large leeks
200 g smoked tofu
2 tbsp olive oil, plus a drizzle
1 large pinch of raw cane sugar or panela
200 ml plant-based cream
2 tbsp malted yeast
1 tsp onion granules
1 tsp mustard
1 tbsp breadcrumbs
Salt, pepper

Discard the toughest green part of the leeks, cut them in half lengthwise, then into small pieces and rinse well in a large bowl of cold water, then drain.

Cut the tofu into small pieces the size of lardons. Fry for 5 minutes in a frying pan with 1 tablespoon of olive oil, or until golden brown.

Empty the pan, add the remaining olive oil and fry the leeks with the pinch of sugar for 10 minutes, or until soft and starting to caramelise. Season with salt and pepper.

To cook the crozets, follow the instructions on the packet, then drain well.

In the meantime, mix the cream with the malted yeast, the onion and mustard, and season with salt and pepper.

Mix the crozets with the cream, add the leeks and lardons and pour into a gratin dish or small ramekins. Sprinkle with breadcrumbs and a drizzle of olive oil. Bake for about 25 minutes, or until the gratin is lovely and golden. Serve immediately.

Comment

Crozets can either be made from 100% buckwheat or with wheat, but the latter often contain eggs.

Soba noodles, shiitake and spring onions

Soba noodles are one of my favourites, especially the 100% buckwheat ones. They're much better when rinsed under cold water after cooking and then reheated immediately afterwards by covering them with vegetable stock. They're absolutely delicious in this recipe with a hazelnut butter sauce.

Serves 4
Prep time: 25 minutes
Cooking time: 10 minutes

400 g soba noodles
400 g shiitake mushrooms
2 tbsp olive oil
1 level tbsp hazelnut butter
2 heaped tsp white miso
1½ tsp tamari
2-3 spring onions, depending on their size
Salt, pepper

Heat a large saucepan of water for cooking the soba noodles.

In the meantime, quickly clean the mushrooms with a clean cloth without washing them, and cut off any earthy or hard stem ends. Fry the mushrooms in olive oil over a high heat for about 10 minutes, or until cooked through and slightly browned. Season with salt and pepper and set aside.

Prepare the sauce: mix the hazelnut butter with the miso and tamari. Gradually add just enough water until smooth and creamy but not too thick.

To cook the noodles, follow the instructions on the packet. Drain and run under cold water, stirring with your fingertips. Tip into a dish, add the cream sauce and mushrooms and sprinkle with chopped spring onions.

Rainbow pad Thai

These rice noodles are colourful thanks to a simple trick and then pan-fried with tofu, garlic and ginger. For a really WOW effect, pour a few drops of lemon juice on the blue noodles, which will instantly turn pink.

Serves 4
Prep time: 15 minutes
Cooking time: 15 minutes

1 clove garlic
2.5 cm piece fresh ginger
200 g plain or lacto-fermented tofu
1 piece of red cabbage (roughly 5 cm each side)
2 tsp ground turmeric
300 g white rice noodles
2 tbsp coconut oil
Some colourful raw vegetables for decoration (carrots, kohlrabi, Chioggia beetroot), herbs (fresh coriander, lemon balm, basil, mint, etc.)
Salt

Bring two large saucepans of water to the boil.

In the meantime, peel, degerm and slice the garlic. Peel the ginger and chop into very small pieces. Cut the vegetables into the desired shapes (cubes, spheres made with a melon baller, star- or heart-shaped cookie cutters, etc.). Cut the tofu into small cubes.

When the water comes to the boil, put the red cabbage in one saucepan and the turmeric in the other, together with a little salt in each. Simmer for 5 minutes, then remove the red cabbage. Add half of the noodles to each saucepan and cook following the instructions on the packet.

Meanwhile, heat half of the coconut oil in a wok, put in the garlic and ginger and sauté for 1 minute, then add the tofu and sauté for 3-4 minutes, until golden brown.

Drain the pasta in turn and tip into the wok over the tofu. Mix gently and cook for 1 minute. Decorate with the vegetables and herbs, drizzle with the remaining coconut oil and serve immediately.

Moussaka pasta

This recipe combines two great classics of Mediterranean cuisine: lasagne and moussaka – a traditional Greek dish made with aubergines, tomatoes and minced meat, which I've replaced here with tempeh that's delicious cooked with aubergine. It's even better with fresh basil.

Serves 6
Prep time: 45 minutes
Cooking time: 45 minutes

2 aubergines (about 600 g)
1 yellow onion
1 clove garlic
3 ripe tomatoes (Roma if possible, or vine tomatoes)
200 g plain tempeh
1 tsp thyme or oregano
8 tbsp olive oil
1 tbsp tomato paste
10 lasagne sheets
200 ml plant-based cream
2 level tbsp malted yeast
1 tsp onion granules
1 tbsp lemon juice
2-3 tbsp breadcrumbs
Salt, pepper

Wash the aubergines and cut into thin slices. Put them in a colander, sprinkle with salt and toss them. Leave them to release their water.

Cut the tomatoes into cubes and roughly chop the tempeh. Peel, degerm and chop the garlic. Peel and chop the onion. Brown the garlic and onion in 2 tablespoons of the olive oil, then add the tomatoes and thyme as well as 200 ml of water. Leave to cook over a medium heat for about 10 minutes, stirring from time to time. Add the tomato paste and tempeh and cook for another 5 to 10 minutes, adding a little water if necessary: the sauce should be creamy but not runny.

Rinse the aubergine slices and dry on kitchen paper. Fry in 4 to 5 tablespoons of olive oil, on both sides, until softened and golden. Set aside on kitchen paper.

If necessary, pre-cook the lasagne sheets in a large saucepan of hot water, stirring occasionally to prevent them from sticking together.

In a bowl, mix the plant-based cream with the malted yeast, onion and lemon juice, salt and pepper.

Cover the bottom of an ovenproof dish with 1 tablespoon of olive oil. Place a layer of lasagne on top, then add the aubergines and the tempeh tomato sauce. Repeat the process until all the ingredients are used up. The top layer should be of cream sauce. Sprinkle with breadcrumbs to cover.

Bake for 30 minutes in a preheated oven at 180°C (gas mark 4) and serve hot.

Stir fry Chinese cabbage, ginger and cashew nuts

Stir fry is a Chinese dish made with ingredients cut into small pieces, quickly sautéed in a frying pan and then coated with sauce. Here's a version I really like made with cabbage, quite a lot of ginger and crunchy cashew nuts. For a one-dish meal, add some diced sautéed tofu.

Serves 2
Prep time: 10 minutes
Cooking time: 10 minutes

180 g Chinese noodles
1 clove garlic
2.5 cm piece fresh ginger
½ Chinese cabbage
40 ml tamari or shoyu
2 tbsp sesame oil, plus 1 tbsp
1 tsp maple syrup
2 level tsp arrowroot
10 cashew nuts

To cook the noodles, follow the instructions on the packet, then drain in a colander.

Meanwhile, prepare the sauce: mix the tamari, oil and maple syrup in a bowl. Add the arrowroot and whisk briskly until smooth and there are no lumps. Set aside.

Slice the Chinese cabbage thinly. Heat the tablespoon of sesame oil in a wok or similar pan and put in the peeled, degermed and chopped garlic and the ginger cut into very fine matchsticks. Fry for 1 minute then add the cabbage and cook for 4-5 minutes, stirring constantly. Return the noodles to the wok, add the sauce, mix well and cook for about 3 minutes more, or until the sauce has thickened and coated the ingredients. Sprinkle with coarsely chopped cashew nuts and serve immediately.

Tip

Preferably choose fine Asian-style noodles made from wheat, rice or even buckwheat – my favourite ones for this recipe are brown rice noodles, which cook in just 4 minutes.

Chorba with split peas, mint and vermicelli

Chorba is a typical North African soup, eaten almost daily during Ramadan. There are many variations, but the basic recipe always includes mint and fresh coriander. It also usually includes meat, vegetables and vermicelli or cracked wheat, sometimes chickpeas. This veggie version is made with vermicelli and split peas and can be made all year round with tomatoes from a jar. Feel free to use more herbs and vary the vegetables according to what you have on hand: courgette, aubergine, squash, spinach or why not broccoli florets, for a pretty green version. Use either regular or whole-wheat vermicelli.

Serves 4
Prep time: 15 minutes
Cooking time: 35 minutes

1 red or yellow onion
1 small rib of celery
1 tbsp olive oil
½ bunch of fresh coriander
10 mint leaves
2 tsp paprika
400 g cooked crushed tomatoes (fresh and peeled, or from a jar)
150 g split peas, soaked overnight in cold water if you wish
80 g vermicelli
Salt, pepper

Finely chop the celery. Peel and finely chop the onion and sauté in a cast-iron casserole with the olive oil and celery for 3 minutes, stirring. Add the chopped coriander, 6 mint leaves and the paprika. Season with salt and pepper and fry for 1 minute, then add the tomatoes and 1 litre of water.

Rinse the split peas and add them to the casserole. Mix well, cover and cook for about 30 minutes, or until the split peas are just cooked but still a little firm.

Add the vermicelli and cook for another 5 minutes (or the time indicated on the packet). Decorate with the remaining mint leaves and serve hot.

Butternut mac and cheese

You can't beat the Americans when it comes to comfort food. The proof is in the pudding with one of their signature dishes, macaroni and cheese, a creamy pasta gratin with lashings of creamy cheese. Here's a delicious butternut squash version that's just as easy to make as the original and just as creamy, though considerably lighter. Like all gratin dishes, this mac and cheese is even better reheated the next day.

Serves 6
Prep time: 15 minutes
Cooking time: 1 hour

- 1 butternut squash cut in half lengthwise (about 600 g) or 400 g cooked squash
- 2 tsp olive oil
- 2 cloves garlic
- 50 g cashew nut butter
- 200 ml oat or soya milk
- 1 tsp onion granules
- 20 g malted yeast (4 heaped tbsp)
- 1 tsp apple cider vinegar
- ⅓ tsp nutmeg
- 500 g macaroni or other small pasta
- 1 heaped tbsp breadcrumbs
- Salt, pepper

Preheat the oven to 180°C (gas mark 4).

Place the squash flesh side up on a baking tray lined with greaseproof paper, brush with olive oil and season lightly with salt and pepper. Add the garlic cloves to the baking tray. Bake until the squash is tender all the way through, about 40 minutes. Leave to cool and remove the skin.

Bring a generous amount of water to the boil.

Put the squash in the jar of a blender with the soft garlic cloves (remove the skin), cashew nut butter, plant-based milk, onion granules, malted yeast, vinegar, nutmeg and half a teaspoon of salt. Blend for a long time on the highest setting until smooth. Taste and add a little salt and/or pepper, malted yeast or onion granules to taste.

To cook the pasta, follow the instructions on the packet. Drain and tip it into an ovenproof dish, about 4 cm deep. Add the butternut cream and mix, sprinkle with breadcrumbs. Bake for about 20 minutes, until the breadcrumbs are golden and crispy. Serve hot or keep in the fridge for up to 48 hours and reheat in the oven just before serving.

Variation

You can swap the macaroni, which are not always easy to find, for any small pasta you like – conchigliette are a great alternative.

Miso soup with alphabet pasta

This meal-in-a-bowl soup, ready in just 10 minutes, will keep kids entertained while they get protein from the grains, enzymes from the miso and wonderful minerals from the seaweed. Add a few cubes of firm or flavoured tofu (about 40 grams per person), chopped spring onion or crushed peanuts. I usually use a fairly mild miso to make this soup, but you can of course swap all or part of it with a darker, more flavourful miso – in that case, leave out the tamari. Seaweed flakes can be found in the Asian or spice section of organic food shops, and if you're lucky enough to find vegan dashi stock there, absolutely use it instead of vegetable stock.

For 4 small (or 2 medium) bowls
Prep time: 3 minutes
Cooking time: 10 minutes

1 tsp vegetable stock powder
1 tsp tamari
100 g alphabet pasta
3 tsp dried seaweed flakes
1 tbsp white miso

Mix 600 ml of water with the stock and tamari in a saucepan. Bring to the boil, then add the pasta. Stir and simmer for the time indicated on the packet. Add the seaweed flakes 30 seconds before the end of the cooking time. Remove from the heat and add the miso: you can do this by using a spoon to push it through a fine sieve dipped in water.

Ladle into bowls, adding whatever extra ingredients you feel like.

Spinach pappardelle with creamy hummus sauce

Here's an easy recipe that will make hummus lovers happy: simply mix it with just-cooked vegetables (spinach in this case) and add enough of the pasta cooking water until you have a creamy fragrant sauce. You can, of course, use a ready-made hummus or your favourite recipe (you'll need about 180 grams of hummus), and swap the pappardelle for tagliatelle or another similar pasta. As for the vegetables, choose whatever seasonal vegetables you fancy: cooked squash cubes in winter, fresh tomatoes or courgettes in summer, Brussels sprouts or broccoli in autumn, etc.

Serves 4
Prep time: 20 minutes
Cooking time: 10 minutes

For the hummus:
150 g cooked chickpeas (rinsed if from a jar)
25 g tahini (white sesame butter)
1 tbsp lemon juice
1 small clove garlic
1 heaped tsp ground cumin
½ tsp salt
40 ml olive oil

300 g pappardelle

200 g fresh spinach
1 clove garlic
1 tbsp olive oil
2 tomatoes or 1 large handful of cherry tomatoes
Herbs (optional)

Prepare the hummus: process the chickpeas with 50 ml of water, then add the tahini, lemon juice, the peeled, degermed and crushed garlic, the cumin and salt. Process for a long time, adding the olive oil little by little, until smooth and creamy.

To cook the pasta, follow the instructions on the packet. Keep a cup of the cooking water aside then drain the pasta.

Wash the spinach, remove the hard part of the stems and drain well. Heat the olive oil in a large saucepan together with the peeled, degermed and crushed garlic. Put in the spinach for a few minutes or until wilted, then add the hummus and mix. Pour in a little of the cooking water (about 40 ml) while stirring until the consistency is like light cream. Add the pasta and toss to coat well. Adjust the seasoning if necessary and serve immediately, topped with a few slices of fresh tomato and/or herbs if you wish.

Spaghetti Breton style

Here's a pasta dish that's quite different from spaghetti bolognese and that will appeal to anyone who loves the flavours of the sea. Sea spaghetti have a particularly mild flavour, so if you've never tried fresh seaweed, now is the time. You can find sea spaghetti in the fresh-food section of organic shops and it keeps for weeks in the fridge. When it's time to prepare it, simply immerse in a large bowl of cold water to get rid of the salt and to rehydrate it. Dry-roasted buckwheat gives crunchiness to this dish, while the light cream made with cashew nuts and cider vinegar – that takes a jiffy to make in a blender – evokes Brittany's famous buttermilk but is a plant-based and very silky version of it.

Serves 4
Soaking time: 4 hours
Prep time: 20 minutes
Cooking time: 10 minutes

- 70 g cashew nuts, soaked for 4 hours in abundant cold water
- 100 g sea spaghetti
- 1 pinch sea salt
- 1½ tsp apple cider vinegar
- 400 g spaghetti
- 70 g unhulled buckwheat

Dip the sea spaghetti into a large bowl of cold water and, holding it with your fingertips shake it gently for about 10 seconds. Repeat in clean water and leave for 5 minutes. Rinse and drain, taste the seaweed to make sure it's not too salty. If it is, repeat step two. Set aside.

Bring a generous amount of water to the boil to cook the pasta.

In the meantime, rinse the cashew nuts and blend for a long time with 110 ml of water and the salt (unless you feel the seaweed is salty enough). Add the vinegar and mix.

Dry roast the buckwheat for a few minutes over a medium heat in a frying pan, stirring until nice and golden and it releases a nutty aroma. Set aside off the heat.

To cook the pasta, follow the instructions on the packet. Drain and gently toss with the creamy sauce and the sea spaghetti. Serve immediately with the toasted buckwheat on the side.

Chic Creative Recipes

Conchiglioni with watercress ricotta

Conchiglioni are large pasta shells that can be stuffed. In this recipe, the plant-based ricotta is made with cashew nuts and tofu, with a little watercress for a piquant touch. It's a lovely contrast of flavours and is a pretty colour reminiscent of spring. You can swap the conchiglioni for cannelloni and prepare them in advance: all you have to do before serving is to reheat them gently in the oven with a drizzle of olive oil.

Serves 4
Soaking time: 3-4 hours
Prep time: 20 minutes
Cooking time: 15 minutes

2 shallots
1 clove garlic
1 large bunch of watercress
120 g cashew nuts, soaked for 3-4 hours in abundant cold water
140 g silken tofu
1 tbsp lemon juice
2 tbsp olive oil
250 g large conchiglioni
Salt, pepper

Peel and finely chop the degermed garlic and shallots, then brown them in a saucepan in 1 tablespoon of the olive oil.

Cut the stems off the watercress, wash the leaves, wipe dry with a clean tea towel and put them in the saucepan. Cook for 2 minutes. Set aside.

Rinse the cashew nuts and blend with the tofu, lemon juice, remaining olive oil, ½ teaspoon of salt and a few turns of a pepper mill until still slightly lumpy. Add the watercress and blend in batches to a cream that's not too smooth (it should have the texture of dairy ricotta).

Cook the pasta in a generous amount of boiling water following the instructions on the packet. Drain well and stuff each conchiglione with the watercress ricotta.

Serve immediately.

Variation

For a thicker ricotta, you can swap the silken tofu for firm tofu, adding a little water if necessary (not more than 50 ml) as you blend.

Spaghetti with chanterelles and hazelnut cream sauce

Chanterelles are delicious little mushrooms that are quick and easy to prepare – simply sauté for a few minutes with a little garlic and shallots and serve on a nice plate of pasta. My personal touch: a smooth and fragrant hazelnut cream sauce that changes everything and highlights any autumn or winter vegetables (squash, parsnips, turnips, etc.). Golden chanterelles can be found in most markets; if not then you can, of course, make this recipe with other types of girolles, shiitake or other mushrooms.

Serves 2
Prep time: 20 minutes
Cooking time: About 10 minutes

200 g chanterelles
1 shallot
1 tbsp olive oil
1 clove garlic
160 g spaghetti
30 g hazelnut butter
50 ml liquid plant-based cream
1 pinch of nutmeg
6-8 hazelnuts
1 heaped tsp chopped parsley
Salt, pepper

Bring a generous amount of water to the boil.

In the meantime, sort the chanterelles and clean them gently with kitchen paper or a clean tea towel (don't wash them or they'll get soggy). Trim the ends of the stems. Brown the peeled and finely chopped shallot in the olive oil for 2 to 3 minutes. Add the mushrooms and sauté for another 3 minutes over a medium heat, stirring regularly. Add the peeled, degermed and chopped garlic at the last minute. Season with salt and pepper and keep warm.

Cook the pasta in boiling water following the instructions on the packet.

Prepare the hazelnut sauce: mix the hazelnut butter in a small bowl with the plant-based cream, the nutmeg and 1 pinch of salt.

Drain the pasta and mix it with the hazelnut sauce. Divide between the plates and top with chanterelles, chopped hazelnuts and parsley. Serve immediately.

Farfalle salad with pickled cucumbers and mint

This fresh pasta salad combines the tangy flavour of pickled cucumber with the coolness of mint and the brightness of pink peppercorns. Pickles keep for several weeks in the fridge: if you have any left over, they're also delicious in a green salad or in a sandwich.

Makes 1 jar (about 750 ml)
Prep time: 20 minutes
Cooking time: 2 minutes
Resting time: 1 week

1 small cucumber (about 300 g)
1 spring onion
1 tsp pink peppercorns
1 tsp coarse sea salt
10 basil leaves
60 g raw cane sugar
300 ml cider vinegar

Serves 4
Prep time: 10 minutes
Cooking time: 10 minutes

400 g farfalle (or rotini, penne, etc.)
1 tbsp rapeseed oil
1 jar pickled cucumbers
4 sprigs fresh mint
1 tbsp pink peppercorns
Salt, pepper

Cucumber pickle with basil

Wash the cucumber. If the skin is thick or you're using a noa cucumber, peel it vertically making stripes. Cut it into slices about 2 mm thick. Quickly wash the basil and gently dry it. Slice the spring onion to halfway up the green part. Put the pink peppercorns in a jar, then add the cucumber, spring onion, basil and salt, interspersing them and squeezing everything to within 2 to 3 cm of the rim.

Pour the vinegar and sugar into a saucepan and simmer for 2 minutes. Pour it over the cucumber to cover and close the jar. Leave to cool and wait a few days before tasting.

Farfalle salad

To cook the pasta, follow the instructions on the packet. Drain and mix with the rapeseed oil. Add the washed and dried mint leaves and the pink peppercorns and season with salt and pepper. Serve with the pickles on the side, in their own jar, so that everyone can take as many as they like.

Butternut squash, red lentil and turmeric ravioli

These pretty homemade ravioli are filled with a very silky cream that's packed with complete proteins. This recipe makes two large portions. These ravioli freeze well; when you cook them, just put them into boiling water and cook for an extra minute.

Serves 2 to 3
Prep time: 50 minutes
Cooking time: 30 minutes
Resting time: 30 minutes

Ravioli dough:
220 g T65 wheat flour, plus a little for dusting
50 g arrowroot powder
½ tsp salt
2 tsp olive oil

Filling:
300 g butternut squash flesh
2 tsp coconut oil
1 scant tsp cumin seeds
150 g red lentils
1 tsp ground turmeric powder (or fresh and grated)
1 tsp ground ginger (or fresh and grated)
Salt, pepper

Prepare the dough: mix the flour, arrowroot and salt in a bowl, make a well in the centre and add the olive oil and 50 ml of water. Mix with a spoon, then add about 100 ml of water little by little while kneading by hand, until a soft but not sticky ball of dough forms. Cover the bowl with a clean tea towel and leave to rest for about 30 minutes.

Prepare the filling: cut the butternut squash flesh into small cubes of about 1.5 cm. Heat the coconut oil in a cast-iron casserole or heavy-bottomed saucepan, add the cumin and heat for 1 minute, then add the squash and fry for about 5 minutes, stirring occasionally.

Add the red lentils and 200 ml of water. Cover tightly and leave to cook over a very low heat for 20 minutes, adding a little water during cooking if necessary.

When the squash and lentils are soft, add the ginger and turmeric, season with salt and pepper and blend until smooth.

Divide the ravioli dough into three balls. Roll the first ball as thinly as possible on a lightly floured worktop and cut out circles with a cookie cutter. Lightly moisten the edges with a finger or brush, place a teaspoon of the butternut squash filling in the centre and fold each circle over, pressing to seal the edges. Do the same with the other two balls of dough. Cook the ravioli in a generous amount of boiling water for about 2 minutes, removing them with a skimmer. Do this in batches to prevent the ravioli from sticking together. Serve very hot.

Tip

If you end up with too much butternut cream filling, freeze it in a silicone muffin tin: reheated with a little water, it makes a delicious satisfying soup.

Black pasta, roasted pumpkin and sage

This beautiful pumpkin surprise is filled with amazing charcoal-coloured black tagliatelle, orange-roasted squash cubes and crispy sage leaves. A veritable party dish, ideal for Halloween.

Serves 4
Prep time: 20 minutes
Cooking time: 30 minutes

1 large pumpkin, about 2 kg, or several small ones
Juice of ½ an orange
1 tsp lemon juice
4 tbsp olive oil
1 clove garlic
12 fresh sage leaves
300 g charcoal tagliatelle (see p. 18)
Salt, pepper

Preheat the oven to 180°C (gas mark 4).

Wash the pumpkin, cut off the top and scoop out the seeds with a spoon. Scoop out the flesh leaving a 1-cm wall all round, and do the same with the cut-off top. Cut the larger pieces into 1-cm cubes and put in a bowl (you should have about 500 grams of flesh). Set the scooped-out pumpkin aside.

Mix the orange and lemon juices, 2 tablespoons of the olive oil, the peeled, degermed and crushed garlic clove, ½ teaspoon of salt and a few turns of the pepper mill in a small bowl. Pour this over the pumpkin cubes and mix well. Spread in a single layer on a baking tray lined with greaseproof paper. Bake for about 20 minutes, until tender and lightly browned. Keep warm in the turned off oven.

Cook the tagliatelle in a generous amount of boiling salted water, then drain. Mix in the saucepan with a drizzle of olive oil and 1 pinch of salt. Fry the sage leaves for a few moments in the remaining olive oil in a frying pan, then set them aside on a sheet of kitchen paper. Tip the pasta into the scooped out pumpkin, add the sage and roasted pumpkin flesh, mix gently and serve immediately.

Orecchiette, rhubarb and garden herbs

If you like creative and offbeat cooking, this recipe is for you. Contrary to popular belief, rhubarb is fabulous in savoury dishes, enhancing them with a pleasant hint of acidity. I've paired it here with balsamic vinegar; it's a really successful combination to which I've added a little maple syrup for sweetness and a touch of Espelette pepper to liven up the dish. Last but not least, a nice bunch of herbs for freshness and extra vitamins. Don't peel the rhubarb; its reddish outer layer disappears when it's cooked and it'll give the dish a pretty pink colour, making it look lovely. Try swapping the balsamic vinegar for lemon juice, and decorate the plate with a few edible flowers or even fresh thyme flowers, if you can find them. A true image of spring...

Serves 4
Prep time: 15 minutes
Cooking time: 25 minutes

250 g rhubarb (1 large stalk)
1 red onion
1 clove garlic
1 tbsp olive oil
½ tbsp maple syrup
2 tbsp balsamic vinegar
1 pinch Espelette pepper
350 g orecchiette pasta
1 bunch of the herbs of your choice (basil, mint, tarragon, oregano, savory, chives, etc.)
Salt, pepper

Wash the rhubarb and cut it into 2 to 3 cm chunks (there's no need to peel it). Chop the peeled onion and the peeled and degermed garlic clove, and brown them in the olive oil. Add the rhubarb, maple syrup and balsamic vinegar. Cover and cook for about 15 minutes over a medium-low heat, stirring occasionally and adding a little water if the mixture sticks or dries out too much. Add salt, pepper, Espelette pepper and blend to the consistency you like.

To cook the pasta, follow the instructions on the packet. Drain and mix with the rhubarb cream and herbs.

Gnocchi alla Romana with spaghetti squash

When I was little, my grandmother used to make me her gnocchi alla Romana: big buttery semolina discs, covered with tomato sauce and grated cheese. I loved it, and for a long time I thought it was the only gnocchi recipe that existed. This is my revisited and 100% veggie version: I've used spaghetti squash, with its curious texture, instead of wheat semolina. The polenta is optional, but it adds a crispiness and a pretty golden contrast to the tomato sauce. Make it to share with your grandmother.

Serves 4
Prep time: 20 minutes
Cooking time: 50 minutes

- 1 spaghetti squash, about 1.2 kg
- 7 tsp olive oil
- 400 g peeled and crushed tomatoes, fresh or canned
- 1 generous pinch of raw cane sugar
- 1 level tsp dried thyme
- 1 tsp balsamic vinegar
- ⅓ tsp garlic powder
- 2 tsp polenta
- Salt, pepper

Preheat the oven to 180°C (gas mark 4).

Cut the squash in half lengthwise and remove the seeds with a spoon. Drizzle the flesh with 2 teaspoons of the olive oil and sprinkle over 1 pinch of salt. Turn the squash halves over and place them flesh-side down on a baking tray. Roast for about 30 minutes, then leave to cool out of the oven.

Meanwhile, put the crushed tomatoes in a saucepan with the sugar, thyme and vinegar, add ½ a level teaspoon of salt and simmer for 30 minutes, partially covered to avoid splatters, stirring occasionally.

Scrape the flesh of the squash with a fork, shredding it to obtain small spaghetti, and put them in a bowl. Gently mix with 3 teaspoons of the olive oil, the garlic powder, ½ teaspoon of salt and a few turns of the pepper mill.

Use a fork to make small nests of spaghetti squash and place them side by side in an ovenproof dish. Hollow out the centre and put in 1 tablespoon of tomato, then sprinkle with a little polenta and drizzle with the remaining olive oil. Bake for 20 minutes and serve hot.

Linguine, asparagus tempura and lemon misonnaise

The secret of tempura batter's lightness is the contrast between the heat of the frying oil and that of the batter made at the last minute with ice-cold water. Here's a version with crispy asparagus, served with beautiful linguine and a miso variation of my favourite mayonnaise.

Serves 4
Prep time: 30 minutes
Cooking time: 20 minutes

20 green asparagus spears
3 tbsp cashew butter
1 heaped tbsp white miso
6 tbsp soya yoghurt
1 tsp organic lemon zest
3 tsp lemon juice
50 g T80 wheat flour
50 g brown rice flour
Oil for frying
2 tbsp olive oil
500 g linguine or long pasta of your choice
Salt, pepper

Several hours in advance, place a jug of water and ice cubes in the fridge.

Wash the asparagus, cut off the hardest part of the stalks and peel up to within 1 cm of the tips. Steam them for about 10 minutes: they should be cooked through but still firm.

Meanwhile, prepare the misonnaise: mix the cashew nut butter, miso and soya yoghurt in a small bowl. Add the zest and 2 tablespoons of lemon juice, season with a little salt and set aside in the fridge.

Bring a large saucepan of water to the boil to cook the pasta.

Prepare the tempura: heat an oil suitable for high-heat frying in a frying pan or sauté pan: there should be at least ½ cm of oil in the pan. Pour 100 ml of the iced water into a soup plate. Mix half of each of the two flours and sift over the water in the soup plate. Stir very lightly with a fork (don't mix, there should be lumps of flour left). Roll half the asparagus in the batter and put them into the pan, without overlapping them. Fry for a few minutes, until the batter is golden, then turn them over and fry for a few more minutes. Drain on kitchen paper. Repeat with the remaining asparagus, making a new batch of batter.

When the pasta is cooked, drain and mix with the olive oil and the remaining lemon juice, salt and pepper. Transfer to a dish or directly to individual plates. Top with the asparagus tempura and serve with the misonnaise.

Rice paper ravioli, lacto-fermented tofu, herbs and flowers from the garden

> *These very elegant ravioli are filled with lacto-fermented tofu with the flavour of fresh cheese, and herbs and flowers from the garden. Enjoy them as an appetiser, a chic aperitif or even as a main course with a large mixed salad.*

Makes 12 ravioli
Prep time: 30 minutes
Cooking time: 15 minutes

200 g lacto-fermented tofu
2 tbsp sesame oil
2 heaped tsp white miso
Zest of ½ a lemon
1 tbsp lemon juice
2 level tbsp of your choice of herbs (chives, parsley, mint, basil, tarragon, fresh coriander, etc.) or small edible flowers
A few leaves or flowers for decorating
12 small rice paper wrappers
Salt, pepper

Mash or coarsely blend the tofu with 1 tablespoon of the sesame oil, the miso, lemon zest and juice, salt and pepper. Finely chop the herbs and add them to the mixture along with the flowers.

Soak 1 rice wrapper in cold water and place it on a lightly oiled plate. Let the wrapper rehydrate for a few moments, then place a few leaves and decorative flowers in the centre and cover with 1 tablespoon of the tofu mixture, pressing down to form a square about 5 cm on each side. Gently fold the rice wrapper over the tofu to form a square (be careful not to tear the wrapper). Repeat with the remaining tofu, rice wrappers, leaves and flowers, then fry the ravioli in a non-stick frying pan with the remaining sesame oil for 3 to 4 minutes on each side over a medium heat. The ravioli should be crisp without browning too much. Serve hot or warm.

Tip

To go faster, I put three oiled plates on my worktop and put the wet rice wrappers on them as I go along; that way they rehydrate while I fill the ones that are ready. If the leaves dry out too quickly, brush lightly with a little water.

Mafaldine pasta, crispy aubergine and sesame mayonnaise

> *We're often stuck when it comes to cooking aubergines and it's a pity because they lend themselves to many delicious recipes. Here, I've chosen a healthy and light way of frying by using a polenta and plant-based milk batter to give them a deliciously crispy melt-in-the-mouth texture. They don't end up saturated with oil as is too often the case when cooking them (aubergines are like sponges). A fool-proof mayonnaise – that's incredibly like the real thing – provides a great creamy contrast, while the basil and lemon add a touch of freshness. Use a serrated knife to cut the aubergines as it makes the job easier. Cut into very thin slices so that they cook all the way through.*

Serves 4
Prep time: 25 minutes
Cooking time: 10 minutes

- 2 large aubergines
- 4 tbsp olive oil
- 150 ml plant-based milk (soya, oat, etc.)
- 4-6 tbsp breadcrumbs
- Fleur de sel
- 400 g mafaldine or other similar pasta (rotini, farfalle, etc.)
- 1 heaped tbsp cashew butter
- 1 heaped tbsp tahini
- 4 tbsp plant-based yoghurt (coconut, soya)
- 1 scant tsp mustard
- Zest of ½ a lemon
- 2 tsp lemon juice
- 10 basil leaves
- Salt, pepper

Wash the aubergines and slice them into very thin rounds (a serrated knife is best). Heat half of the olive oil in a large frying pan over a medium heat. Pour the milk into a soup plate and put the polenta in another one. Dip half of the aubergine slices in the milk and then in the polenta and brown them on both sides in the olive oil until golden brown; they should be crispy on the outside and tender in the middle. Repeat with the remaining aubergine slices. Set them aside on kitchen paper and sprinkle with fleur de sel.

To cook the pasta, follow the instructions on the packet, then drain.

Mix the cashew butter and tahini with the plant-based yoghurt in a small bowl until smooth. Add the mustard, lemon zest and juice and mix. Season with salt and pepper. Pour the sauce over the pasta and toss gently, then add the fried aubergine slices and basil leaves. Serve immediately or keep in the fridge to enjoy as a salad (in which case, add the basil at the last moment).

Pink pasta with beetroot cream and purslane

This incredibly simple recipe is a hit with kids and adults alike: the beetroot cream sauce gives the spaghetti a beautiful pale pink colour. The more sauce you add, the more intense the colour. It's up to you how much to use – you can always serve the rest of the sauce in a separate bowl. I suggest you serve this pasta with crisp, delicate purslane leaves that will enhance the pinkness of the dish, but you can also use spinach leaves, rocket or watercress. If you wish, you can serve this dish with oven-roasted walnuts for a pleasant contrast of textures and flavours. Good to know; this sauce is also delicious cold in a pasta salad.

Serves 4
Prep time: 15 minutes
Cooking time: 10 minutes

230 g cooked beetroot
110 g silken tofu
1 tbsp walnut oil
1 generous pinch of paprika
400 g spaghetti or tagliatelle
2 large handfuls purslane
Salt, pepper

Blend the beetroot with the tofu, oil, paprika, salt and pepper until smooth and creamy.

To cook the pasta, follow the instructions on the packet. Keep a cupful of the cooking water, then drain the pasta. Mix with the beetroot cream sauce, adding a little of the cooking water if necessary so that the sauce coats the pasta well. Rinse the purslane quickly and dry gently with a clean tea towel. Mix it with the pasta at the last moment and serve immediately.

Tip

Try serving this dish with oven-roasted walnuts: spread 50 g of walnuts on a baking tray and bake for 8 minutes at 180°C (gas mark 4). Chop coarsely and sprinkle over the pasta or serve separately in a bowl.

Sweet potato gnocchi

These pretty gluten-free gnocchi are served with a creamy, silky chestnut and hazelnut sauce. It's best to slow cook the sweet potato in the oven until soft and no longer watery and, if you wish, swap the oat flour for finely ground flakes or any other flour you like.

Serves 2
Prep time: 20 minutes
Cooking time: 10 minutes

300 g oven-roasted sweet potato, warm (see tip below)
50 g wholemeal rice flour plus a little for dusting
40 g oat flour (gluten free if you wish)
30 g arrowroot powder
½ tsp salt
1 large handful of spinach leaves
Olive or coconut oil

For the sauce:
100 g cooked chestnuts (plain, with no other added ingredients)
Juice of ½ an orange
2 tsp hazelnut butter
1 tsp tamari
½ tsp vegetable stock powder
Salt, pepper

Mix the flours with the arrowroot and salt, make a well in the centre and put in the peeled and mashed sweet potato. Mix by hand until you have a smooth ball of dough; don't work it too much or the dough will become sticky. Cut into four portions. Dust a worktop with flour and roll each piece of dough into a rope about 1.5 cm in diameter, then cut into small pieces 2 cm long. Roll them, if you like, over the tines of a fork to give them their characteristic shape and set them aside.

Bring a large saucepan of salted water to the boil and cook the gnocchi in batches for a few minutes, until they rise to the surface. Remove them as you go with a skimmer and place them on a large plate. Sauté the gnocchi for a few minutes in a non-stick frying pan in a little olive or coconut oil.

Prepare the sauce: heat 100 ml of water with the stock, then blend for a long time with the chestnuts, orange juice, hazelnut butter and tamari. Season with salt and pepper and adjust the amount of water according to the desired texture.

Serve the gnocchi hot with the spinach leaves and chestnut cream.

Tip

To slow cook sweet potatoes; score the skin deeply with a sharp knife and place them on a baking tray. Bake at 190°C (gas mark 5) until the flesh is perfectly tender in the middle (30 minutes to 1 hour depending on their size). You can make a large batch and freeze them when they're cool. For the 300 g required for this recipe, use about 350 g of raw sweet potato.

Rice tagliatelle, black garlic, courgettes and preserved lemon

Light, fresh and refined, these pretty tagliatelle are ideal for a summer dinner. Black garlic is a real treat with its melt-in-the-mouth texture and sweet-tart flavour – if you can't find it, use garlic cloves roasted in the oven.

Serves 4
Prep time: 25 minutes
Cooking time: 10 minutes

500 g white or semi-wholegrain rice tagliatelle (or noodles)
800 g long courgettes
2 tbsp olive oil
2 tbsp sesame oil
2 tsp lemon juice
2 tsp tamari
6 cloves black garlic
1 preserved lemon
Salt
Mint or basil (optional)

Wash the courgettes, peel with a vegetable peeler to make stripes, then cut into tagliatelle until you reach the seeds in the middle of the courgettes.

Bring a generous amount of water to the boil to cook the pasta.

Put the courgette tagliatelle in a sauté pan or large saucepan with a little water and the olive oil in the bottom. Cover tightly and cook over a medium heat for 5 minutes, or until just tender. Remove the lid and set them aside. In a small bowl, mix the sesame oil, lemon juice and tamari. Peel the garlic cloves and finely slice them. Take the skin of the preserved lemon and cut it into small dice.

To cook the pasta, follow the instructions on the packet. Drain and add the courgettes and the sesame oil seasoning, garlic and preserved lemon. Season lightly with salt and mix very gently.

Serve immediately with a little mint or basil if you wish.

Index of Recipes

All raw lasagne, 68

Almond and basil pesto, 27

Autumn minestrone, cauliflower, chestnuts and Jerusalem artichokes, 58

Black pasta, roasted pumpkin and sage, 124

Butternut mac and cheese, 106

Butternut squash, red lentil and turmeric ravioli, 122

Cannelloni, chard and soya curds, 38

Cashew cream, 28

Chickpea flour trofie, 14

Chorba with split peas, mint and vermicelli, 104

Colourful pasta, 18

Conchigliette and caramelised shallots gratin, 46

Conchigliette, slow-cooked fennel, pomegranate and baby leaf spinach, 82

Conchiglioni with watercress ricotta, 116

Courgetti, roasted garlic and smoked paprika, 62

Egg-free pasta, 7

Farfalle with wild garlic pesto, hemp and baby radishes, 66

Farfalle salad, with pickled cucumbers and mint, 120

Fettuccine Alfredo, 48

Fried noodles al'arrabiata, 52

Garlic croutons, 26

Gnocchi alla Romana with spaghetti squash, 128

Gremolata, 30

Linguine, asparagus tempura and lemon misonnaise, 130

Linguine with kale and pumpkin seed pesto, 80

Linguine alla puttanesca, 40

Mafaldine pasta, crispy aubergine and sesame mayonnaise, 134

Mafaldine pasta with sage, fresh broad beans and crunchy almonds, 64

Miso soup with alphabet pasta, 108

Moussaka pasta, 100

Mung bean, avocado and lime orecchiette salad, 76

Mushroom risoni risotto, 50

One pot coco-curry pasta, 92

One pot 'cheesy broccoli' pasta, 72

Orecchiette, rhubarb and garden herbs, 126

Pink pasta with beetroot cream and purslane, 136

Plant-based Parmesan, 24

Quinoa and lemon lasagne, 16

Rainbow Pad Thai, 98

Ramen, caramelised tempeh and orange-glazed carrots, 90

Real gnocchi di patate, 12

Rice paper ravioli, lacto-fermented tofu, herbs and flowers from the garden, 132

Rice tagliatelle, black garlic, courgettes and preserved lemon, 140

Roasted chickpeas, 29

Roasted tomato sauce, 25

Savoyard gratin with crozets, leeks and smoked tofu 'lardons', 94

Shirataki express, red onion, fresh coriander and peanuts, 84

Skillet lasagne, roasted tomatoes and white bean béchamel, 42

Soba noodles, shiitake and spring onions, 96

Spaghetti with chanterelles and hazelnut cream sauce, 118

Spaghetti, seitan 'meatballs' and tomato sauce, 36

Spaghetti bolognese, 44

Spaghetti carbonara with aubergine 'bacon', 54

Spaghetti Breton style, 112

Spelt tagliatelle, 10

Spinach pappardelle with creamy hummus sauce, 110

Stir fry Chinese cabbage, ginger and cashew, 102

Sweet potato gnocchi, 138

Sweet potato spaghetti with caramelised orange, 78

Tamari toasted seeds, 32

Torsade, roasted pepper cream and basil, 74

Tri-coloured tagliatelle, vegetables and white miso cream sauce, 86

Trofiette al ragù, 56

Trofiette, poivrade artichokes, rocket and sunflower 'pine nuts', 70

Vegetable noodles, 20

Walnut pesto, 31

White bean béchamel sauce, 33

Index of Ingredients

Almonds, 27, 32, 64, 68, 74, 80
Artichoke, Jerusalem, 58
Artichoke, poivrade, 70
Asparagus, 130
Aubergine, 54, 100, 134
Avocado, 68, 76

Basil, 27, 74
Beetroot, 18, 136
Blueberries, 18
Brazil nuts, 24
Broccoli, 18, 72
Butternut squash, 18, 106, 122

Cannelloni, 38
Capers, 40
Carrots, 18, 86, 90
Cashew nuts, 24, 27, 28, 32, 48, 54, 66, 68, 86, 102, 106, 112, 116, 130
Cauliflower, 48, 58
Chanterelles, 118
Charcoal, 18
Chard, 38
Chestnuts, 58, 138
Chick pea flour, 14
Chick peas, 29, 110
Chinese cabbage, 102
Conchigliette, 46, 82
Conchiglioni, 116
Coriander, fresh, 76, 84
Courgettes, 62, 68, 86, 92, 140
Crozets, 94
Cucumber, 120
Curry powder, 92

Dulse, 40

Farfalle, 66, 120
Fennel, 82
Fettuccine, 48

Garlic, 26, 27, 30

Garlic, black 140
Garlic, wild, 66
Gnocchi, 12, 128

Hazelnuts, 118
Hemp seeds, 66, 68

Kale, 80
Kidney beans, 36

Lasagne, 16, 42, 100
Leeks, 94
Lentils, green, 56
Lentils, red, 122
Linguine, 40, 80, 130

Macaroni, 106
Mafaldine, 64, 134
Mint, 104
Miso, 86, 90, 108, 130, 132
Mung beans, 76
Mushrooms, 50

Noodles, 102
Noodles, Asian, 52
Noodles, vegetable, 20

Olives, 40
Orecchiette, 76, 126

Pappardelle, 110
Parmesan, plant-based, 24
Parsley, 30, 31
Penne, 74, 92
Pomegranate, 82
Potatoes, 12
Pumpkin seeds, 80
Pumpkin, 124
Purslane, 136

Quinoa, 16

Radishes, 66
Ramen, 90
Ravioli, 122
Red cabbage, 98

Red pepper, 52, 74
Rhubarb, 126
Rice noodles, 98, 140
Rice wrappers, 132
Ricotta, 116
Risoni (orzo), 50
Rocket, 70
Rotini, 74

Sage, 64, 124
Seaweed, 112
Seiten, 36
Sesame, 134
Shallots, 46, 50, 54, 58
Shirataki, 84
Shitake mushrooms, 96
Soba noodles, 96
Spaghetti squash, 128
Spaghetti, 36, 44, 54, 112, 118, 136
Spelt flour, 10
Spinach, 18, 82, 110, 138
Split peas, 104
Spring onions, 96
Sunflower seeds, 32, 38, 42, 70
Sweet potato, 78, 138

Tagliatelle, 10, 56, 86, 124, 136
Tamari, 32
Tempeh, 90, 100
Tofu, 46, 52, 94, 98, 116, 132, 136
Tomatoes, 25, 36, 42, 44, 52, 68, 100, 104, 110, 128
Trofie, 14
Trofiette, 56, 70
Turmeric, 18

Vermicelli, 104

Walnuts, 31
Watercress, 116
White beans, 33, 42, 58